Date Due

QUEBEC: Bonjour, eh?

A PRIMER FOR ENGLISH-SPEAKERS

by

Heather Keith-Ryan

and

Sharon McCully

illustrations by **Christine Hunt**
maps by **Wendy Lewis**

SHELTUS & PICARD

First publication 1996

Canadian Cataloguing in Publication Data:

Keith-Ryan, Heather, 1940–
Quebec: bonjour, eh? : a primer for English-speakers

ISBN 0-9696296-2-1

1. Quebec (Province)–Description and travel.
I. McCully, Sharon, 1948– II. Title.

FC2917.5.K43 1996 917.1404′4 C96-900157-6
F1052.K43 1996

Illustrations by Christine Hunt. Maps by Wendy Lewis.
174 pages. 11 cm x 18 cm (4.25″ x 7″).

Cover illustration by Christine Hunt
Photograph of Heather Keith-Ryan by Jane Hamilton
Printed and bound in Canada by AGMV, Montreal, Quebec

Sheltus & Picard Inc.
PO Box 1321, Bedford, Quebec, Canada
J0J 1A0

DEDICATION

This book is dedicated to all the English-speaking Quebecers who are still here, still talking, still working to build bridges with their fellow Quebecers whose first language is French.

And to Heather's children Tom, Colin, Kevin, Michaela and Shannon Ryan.

And to Sharon's mom Marie O'Keeffe, husband Ralph and children Tara, Aaron, Andrew, Leslie and Matthew.

ACKNOWLEDGEMENTS

This primer could not have been created without the help of many people. To all those who settled some question of usage or fact we offer our thanks: you are too many to name! We both appreciate the encouragement of our families and friends, who have been urging us to get this book out for a long time. And especially we thank our most assiduous critic and editor, Heather's daughter Shannon Ryan; our American friends who made many useful suggestions for things Americans might want to know: Wendy and Ted Peskin, Susan Gordon, and Heather's daughter-in-law, the other Shannon Ryan. For vital help with the French language we thank our French-language critics and assistants Gérard Normandin, Patrick and Marthe McDonald, Louise Clostre and Louise Landry Balas. Here and there we disregarded their advice and went our own way;* any errors are ours. We have had help from Madeleine Keith, a direct descendant of the seigneur of Trois Pistoles. We also thank Peter White. Gordon Rowe and Anthony Thomson, the owners of Immeubles Stuart R.T. in Knowlton, Quebec, and our colleagues at Stuart

---

*Our pronunciation system, for instance, is our own. We wanted sounds an English-speaker could pronounce immediately without studying vowels not found in English, but which could be understood by **les Québécois**. We hope to hear from you to find out if we hit it!

and *The Record* have been endlessly accommodating to writers' schedules. Thanks also to Ann Edwards, Jane Hamilton, and Joan Taylor; and to Sandy Wolofsky, who started with us in Quebec and went to seek her fortune in Russia. We'd like to thank in a special way two friends of Heather's children who became an integral part of this project: Christine Hunt, who drew the illustrations, and Wendy Lewis, who came through with the maps.

Sharon says: This book would not have been written were it not for the dogged persistence of my partner and friend Heather whose abiding sense of duty forced me to give up warm days at the beach and cool nights by the fire to share this vision of Quebec.

We also thank Henry and Jean St Gelais of Informatique First Byte, who endured our lack of expertise in the world of computer graphics with smiles and grace; and our editors and publishers Ashley Sheltus and Charlotte Picard, who offered suggestions and advice at every level.

Thank you all!

TABLE OF CONTENTS

QUEBEC: Bonjour, eh?

A PRIMER FOR ENGLISH-SPEAKERS

BIENVENUE AU QUÉBEC!

Welcome to **la belle province,** where language is legislated, politics are potent, and the majority of folks are French and friendly.

We have written this thumbnail sketch of Quebec from the perspective of two English-speaking women—here referred to as anglophones—each the mother of five children. We are Quebecers, as proud of this province as any other **Québécois.** We will provide you with just enough information to stimulate a healthy curiosity and desire to discover us and our home–**notre chez-nous.** We feel it is important to show the playful, wondrous side of Quebec rarely shown in the media. We also want to extend an invitation—or an olive branch—and urge you to visit us.

It's no secret there are different political ideologies among Quebecers and divergent views on how Quebec's goals can best be achieved. It is important to remember, however, that 1992 marked the 350th anniversary of the founding of Montreal, as well as the 125th anniversary of the Canadian Confederation, and Quebecers of all stripes continue to live in relative harmony. In the shops and on the streets, Quebecers spend very little time talking about Canada's constitutional quagmire.

You may have read and heard about Quebec's penchant for power-politics and poll-reading, but the first numbers most Quebecers check in the morning are the winning numbers in the Loto 6/49. Then, depending on the season, we check the sports news to see if **les Canadiens** trounced **les Maple Leafs** (in hockey), or whether **les Expos** are doing better than **les Blue Jays** (in baseball).

We offer some basic French words and expressions to enhance your visit to this predominantly French-speaking environment. To do this, we've employed a primitive method of language instruction: point, shrug, and the magic word. Show us a two-year old who can't clear a path to the toilet when he says "pee-pee". As with the tots, we've put the onus on the person listening to understand.

We include an anglicized pronunciation guide to make you feel bilingual and help get you out of a tough spot. We recommend you leave the phrase "I don't speak French" at home and prepare to have some fun. If you do, we'll share one of the country's best-kept secrets: many Quebecers speak English as well as you do, and the rest can point, smile, and count in our mother tongue. But you shouldn't come to Quebec without trying to speak a little French.

If this is a first visit, you'll discover the zest for living–**la joie de vivre** that makes Quebec different from all the other Canadian provinces. You will find that Quebecers–**les Québécois** and **Québécoises** like to party. We celebrate pigs, hydro-electricity, jazz, cowboys, and all kinds of things; but the biggest party of all happens on the feast day of St. John the Baptist, June 24, **la fête nationale.**

Don't be surprised if nearby groups break into a chorus or two of Gilles Vigneault's **"Gens du Pays" (gens** are the people and **le pays** is the country). Although it's the unofficial national anthem of Quebec, it also doubles as Quebec's "Happy Birthday" song, and the event is more likely to be a birthday party than a political rally.

It's easy to confuse Quebec province–**la province du Québec** with Quebec City–**la ville de Québec.** We recall waiting at Mirabel airport west of Montreal for a young man to arrive from France, only to discover he had landed in Quebec City, some 250 kilometers (155 mi.) away! But, hey, **c'est la vie!**

Whether you are heading to a Laurentian ski resort, a snowmobile excursion in northern Quebec, a dog-sledding adventure with the Cree, a whale-watching excursion on the St. Lawrence or a salmon fishing trip in the Gaspé, you will be amazed by the cornucopia of sights and sounds that are distinctly **québécois.** From the antique shops and the sophisticated designer boutiques, to the distinct seventeenth-century architecture of the old cities, or the Matane fisherman who insists you sample his shrimp with your morning coffee, there is much to appreciate.

We will tell you about the Quebec we know, but we want you to come and form your own opinion. Come with an open mind and a willingness to communicate. Let your children, who may have a better knowledge of French than you, have the thrill of communicating in another language.

And once you've savored some of Quebec's treasures, you'll notice that your tongue slips more easily around words and phrases in French too. In fact, you'll find that even the slightest attempt to speak French will bring a positive and pleased response from **les Québécois** you meet.

So, forget politics; relax and enjoy the experience. There are so many more important things to think about when visiting Quebec: like which cheek to put forward first for the standard double-cheek peck. (Usually it's right side first, but watch the other person and cock your head accordingly.) Until you get accustomed to this greeting, it is perfectly acceptable to shake hands.

CHAPTER 1

A DELIBERATELY ABRIDGED HISTORY OF QUEBEC

For some Quebecers, history is a blur before the dawn of the Quiet Revolution–**la Révolution tranquille** in the 1960s. Since then, the nationalist movement, the object of which is to allow the French-speaking majority to become masters of their destinies, **"maîtres chez nous,"** has flourished. The history of Quebec is subject to interpretation by individual Canadians, and the versions taught in Quebec classrooms sometimes vary dramatically. Here is our version.

JACQUES CARTIER, A GREAT EXPLORER

Although his name graces one of the main spans joining the island of Montreal to the mainland, Jacques Cartier had nothing to do with its construction. Cartier was probably no different from most first-time visitors to Quebec. He came looking for one thing, found another, and spent a fair bit of time trying to convince people back home it was not what they might expect.

Cartier and his crew of fifty men set sail from St. Malo, France, on April 20, 1534 under orders from the King of France to explore the New World and find a route to China. After planting a cross and a French flag on the shores of the Gaspé peninsula, Cartier returned to

France with stories of Chinamen in feathers who commuted by canoe instead of rickshaw. He also had with him the sons of Chief Donnacona. He reported to the king that there was much salmon, but no silk.

Cartier returned the following year to retrace his steps up the St. Lawrence River, once again **en route** to China, this time landing near what is now the Montreal suburb of Lachine (China–**La Chine).** History tells us that even in 1535 without benefit of a functioning tourist bureau, bilingual signs, or a common language,

Cartier managed to find his way to the top of Mount Royal–**Mont-Royal** and was so enraptured he vowed to return. He may have had second thoughts after wintering near present-day Quebec City and losing several crew members to scurvy. He didn't return for five years, and his attempts to establish a permanent colony failed.

SAMUEL DE CHAMPLAIN, HERO OF NEW FRANCE

In 1603, Samuel de Champlain came to New France–**la Nouvelle-France,** and in 1608 he founded Quebec City. His name has since been immortalized, appearing on shopping malls, bridges, car dealerships, and a huge lake which straddles the Vermont, New York, and Quebec borders. Champlain was really the first heroic character in the story of **la Nouvelle-France** and remains one of the legendary figures of Quebec history. His lengthy voyages inland, his determination to establish a foothold for his Church and country in the hostile wilderness, his alliances with the natives and his death on Christmas Day, 1635 at his **Habitation** in Quebec City make him worthy of the title Genuine North American Hero.

SETTLING NEW FRANCE

The first attempts by the French to set up a colony in Acadia–**l'Acadie** (now part of Atlantic Canada) in the early 1600s were disappointing, but the later settlement at what is now Quebec City met with better results. Ultimately the King of France agreed to send settlers to claim land along the mighty St. Lawrence River–**le fleuve St-Laurent.** Land grants were apportioned in long thin strips called **seigneuries** at right angles to the river.

Soon after the landlords–**les seigneurs** set up camp in **la Nouvelle-France,** the King's girls or wards–**les**

filles du Roy arrived, and the population of the little colony grew. Priests were dispatched to convert **"les sauvages"** (the indigenous people). Nuns–**les Soeurs** nursed the sick and taught reading, writing and 'rithmetic.

The increasing and multiplying continued until the mid-1950s, with gentle cajoling and the promise of heavenly reward from the Catholic Church. Families with as many as 15 children were not uncommon. As the influence of the Catholic Church waned and the feminist movement waxed, the birth rate nosedived. To address the problem, in the 1980s the Quebec government picked up where the Catholic Church left off and introduced a bonus for women to produce children. More recently, Lucien Bouchard, now premier (prime minister) of Quebec, challenged Quebec women to have more babies to replenish the French-speaking population.

THE INDIGENOUS PEOPLES

When the white man first set foot in North America, the native peoples had been on the continent for an estimated 10,000 years. The three principal groups in the northeast were the Inuit, the Algonquin and the Iroquois. There were many tribes, and their itinerant lifestyles did not produce well defined settlements. The group that gave Champlain and the early settlers trouble for close to a century were the Iroquois, a confederacy of five tribes: the Seneca, Oneida, Onondaga, Cayuga and Mohawk. The Richelieu River valley was their principal territory, but they also travelled well beyond the river.

In 1607 England had established its foothold in North America with the founding of Jamestown (Virginia). Then in 1609 Henry Hudson discovered the Hudson River, which in turn opened new travel routes for the

Dutch, allies of the Iroquois. Champlain had first traded with the Algonquins and the Hurons and won their confidence. A rivalry, if not a war, developed over control of the fur trade between the Iroquois and their Dutch allies on one side, and the Algonquins, Hurons and French on the other.

For close to sixty years there were sporadic outbreaks of violence between the indigenous people and the European settlers all over the territory. The natives were weakened by diseases brought by these colonizers, against which they had no immunity. As the eighteenth century dawned, all factions met at the present-day site of Montreal and, under the benevolent eye of the French governor, signed a truce.

Today the native peoples retain their history and culture on reserves throughout Quebec. The Hurons live at Wendake about 30 km (20 mi.) from Quebec City, and some Mohawks live at Kahnawake and Kanesetake less than an hour by car from Montreal. In eastern Quebec there are reserves occupied by Micmac, Montagnais, Naskapi and Abenaki. The majority of the Cree and the Inuit live in the far north.

Ecological awareness has led to a renewed respect for the customs of the people of the First Nations. The Quebec government has recently restored the original lyrical aboriginal names to many northern villages. Fort George has become Chisasibi. Other tongue twisting names of northern villages are Kuujjuaq, Whapmagoostui, Kuujjuarapik, Inukjuak.

FIGHTING IN NEW FRANCE AND NEW ENGLAND

Colonists and native peoples may have found peace on their common turf but it was short-lived, given the antics across the Atlantic. In Europe between 1702 and

1760 there were three major conflicts—with resultant treaties to divvy up the spoils. Acadia was a pawn in this game, and between 1755 and 1763, some 12,000 French-speaking Acadians were expelled by the British from the lands they had settled, a sad chapter in the history of Canada. The exodus, a great loss to the young colony, benefited the future United States, generating a community of Americans in Louisiana proud of their "Cajun" (Acadian) culture, food and music.

In a battle which lasted little more than half an hour, the French and English took the field in September, 1759 on the Plains of Abraham–**les Plaines d'Abraham.** The former battlefield, **le champ de bataille,** is now a tourist site in Quebec city, an important landmark which signifies victory for the English, defeat for the French. This famous battle resulted in the deaths of both the English general Wolfe and the French leader Montcalm. (Legend has it that neither general's aide

spoke the other's language, and so they negotiated the truce in Gaelic!) In the spring of 1760, as luck would have it, the first reinforcements to arrive at the little settlement at Quebec were from England, and the colony became part of British North America.

English forces took Montreal in September of the same year, and the North American chapter of the Seven Years' War came to an end. The Treaty of Paris, ratified in February 1763, left only the islands of St-Pierre and Miquelon in the hands of France. Fought more than 200 years ago, the battle of the Plains of Abraham was one of the pivotal moments in Canadian history. It is known in French Quebec as the Conquest–**la Conquête.**

COLONIAL TIMES

After a few attempts at direct rule of the newly conquered territory, England, in order to keep the French from joining the rebellious colonies to the south, agreed to the suggestions of the governor of the colony, Sir Guy Carleton, and adopted the Quebec Act in 1774. This Act placed authority in the hands of the governor and an appointed council to which the French were to be admitted without restriction. English criminal law was retained, but French civil law, derived from the Custom of Paris and brought to **la Nouvelle-France** in 1663, was used in all other instances. (The recently updated Civil Code of Quebec, which was first codified in 1866 just prior to Confederation, continues this tradition. The form of the Civil Code was based on the 1804 Code Napoléon.) The **seigneurial** system of land tenure was guaranteed. Freedom of Catholic worship was affirmed along with the right of the Catholic Church to collect tithes or taxes, which the religious leaders appreciated more than the citizens.

By this time, the seeds of the American Revolution had been sprouting, and everything had been done to induce the "Canadiens", the French-speaking settlers, to join the fight against England. In 1775, Benedict Arnold and Ethan Allan recruited a small band of New England farmers and took two major outposts of the colony on Lake Champlain: Fort Ticonderoga and Crown Point. These forts controlled access to the Richelieu River and Montreal. Montreal capitulated to the colonial rebels led by Richard Montgomery in the fall of 1775.

Montgomery then marched his men toward Quebec City, where he expected to join Arnold's forces trekking north through the Maine woods. Undaunted by the onset of winter, the armies of Montgomery and Arnold attacked Quebec on New Year's Eve in a raging snowstorm and were soundly defeated. The following spring, major reinforcements from England arrived at Quebec, and Montreal was retaken. The English were not able to retake Ticonderoga, and the colonies to the south ultimately severed their ties with the mother country and in 1776 became the United States of America.

Colonists loyal to England crossed the new border and came to southern Canada. These "Loyalists" needed land for settlement, which under the Quebec Act was granted by the seigneurial system. To confront this problem as well as the dichotomy of the two language groups, the Constitutional Act was adopted in 1791. The territory of Canada was divided into two regions: Upper Canada–**le Haut-Canada,** which had primarily been settled by English-speaking immigrants and is now part of Ontario, and Lower Canada–**le Bas-Canada,** primarily inhabited by those of French-speaking origin, and part of the present-day Quebec. The areas closest to the American border, being relatively far from **le fleuve St-Laurent,** had not been colonized but remained the home of the Abenaki. Many Loyalists settled in this region which we know today as the Gaspé, Eastern Townships and Montérégie. Many others went to Upper Canada and to what we now know as Atlantic Canada (or the Maritime provinces).

As time went on, the western part of the continent opened up for exploration and fur trading. However, decisions were still being made by governors dispatched from England, prompting the residents, including the French, to demand more autonomy. It is evident that current politicians are not the first to raise this issue.

REBELLIONS IN THE COLONY

The fact that major decisions were being made in London thousands of miles from the colony was but one cause that led to the Rebellions of 1837–38. Louis-Joseph Papineau led **les Patriotes** in Lower Canada, and William Lyon Mackenzie led the uprising in Upper Canada. The rebellions, largely a fight between the "peasants" and the "establishment", failed, but they did result in an extensive study of the colony by Lord Durham. He conducted a one-man commission, travelling around the country taking the pulse of settlers. The Durham report produced in 1839 was a highly contentious document. One of Lord Durham's recommendations was to develop policies to assimilate the French-speaking community. This was to be accomplished by banning the French language from the legislature and uniting the two provinces. The philosophy was "unite and anglicize". The Union Act, uniting the two Canadas into one Province of Canada, was passed in 1840.

Despite directives from England, "real Canadians"—those who actually lived in the colony—and Reformists led by Robert Baldwin from Upper Canada and Louis-Hippolyte LaFontaine from Lower Canada worked together. The legislature of the United Province of Canada was moved from Kingston to Montreal. The Reform party (not to be confused with today's party of the same name led by Preston Manning) took office in March of 1848, and one of the symbolic and contentious pieces of legislation put before it was the Rebellion Losses Bill, drafted to compensate those in Lower Canada for their losses in the Rebellions of 1837. (The citizens of Upper Canada had already received compensation.)

The Rebellion Losses Bill was adopted by the legislature in 1849 and officially accepted by the governor-general, Lord Elgin. After the ceremonial signing of the Bill at the Parliament of the time in **Place d'Youville** in Old Montreal, the British merchants rioted in protest. The legislature was burned but the Reformists stood their ground. The government was moved away from Montreal and alternated for a number of years between Toronto and Quebec City before being established at Bytown, now Ottawa.

THE DOMINION OF CANADA IS BORN

Baldwin and LaFontaine retired in 1851, but their successors, John A. Macdonald of Upper Canada and Georges-Étienne Cartier of Lower Canada, led the colony into a formal confederation in 1867. The constitution of the Dominion of Canada was officially known as the British North America Act (BNA Act)–**l'Acte de l'Amérique du Nord britannique.** The Act united the four provinces of Quebec, Ontario, Nova Scotia, and New Brunswick. Other provinces joined over time.

The document was tucked cozily away in some British safety deposit box for the next 100 years and could only be amended with the approval of the British parliament. The act, now called the Constitution Act, was "repatriated" in 1982, when all provinces except Quebec signed an amended version. The Meech Lake Accord (1989) and the Charlottetown Accord (1992) were two agreements drafted to get Quebec to sign the Constitution but neither one was ratified; and in 1996 Quebec still is not a signatory to the current Canadian Constitution, although it nevertheless applies to Quebecers as well as to the rest of Canada. This is but one of the factors that regularly leads Quebec to threaten to separate from Canada.

Canada is a member of the Commonwealth, and our official head of state is Queen Elizabeth II, who is represented by a Canadian-born Governor General. This is why Her Majesty is featured on Canadian money and postage stamps and new citizens swear an oath to her when they become Canadians. This is also why the federal and provincial governments preface their laws with preambles mentioning the Queen.

For nearly 130 years French and English Canadians have lived together as part of the Canadian federation. In 1969 the government of Canada formally adopted legislation giving official recognition to the country's two official languages, French and English. Slow, but consider the plight of the descendants of Donnacona who greeted Cartier on the shores of the St. Lawrence River 450 years ago. While the native languages are recognized regionally, none are "official" languages of Canada.

WAS LOUIS RIEL A QUEBECER?

By the time of Confederation (1867) there were several thousand settlers west of the Great Lakes, the majority of them **Métis.** The Métis were people of mixed race, many fathered by the **coureurs de bois,** the intrepid Frenchmen who canoed and explored with the native peoples and married native women. Louis Riel was the young, Quebec-educated, charismatic leader of these people, and it was he who negotiated the entrance of Manitoba into Confederation in 1870. How different the history of Canada might have been if Riel had become Manitoba's first premier!

Riel obtained linguistic and religious guarantees for his people, guarantees which were not respected for long. After the execution of an Orangeman (an Irish Protestant) on Riel's orders in 1870, chaos ensued, and Riel exiled himself to the United States. During this time Gabriel Dumont assumed leadership of the Métis and worked on their behalf with the government to settle land claims. Migration west by French-Canadians diminished, but countless other Europeans settled the territory as the railway made its way west.

In 1884 Riel resumed his leadership role, and petitions about the land claims were sent to Ottawa and then on to England. The Métis countered the delaying tactics of the government by setting up a provisional government of their own. A skirmish at Duck Lake frightened Prime Minister John A. Macdonald into sending in the army. Riel was becoming a bit of a religious fanatic and was "hearing voices", not a good sign for the confrontation.

In mid-May 1885 the Battle of Batoche was fought. The greatly outnumbered Métis put up a strong fight but lost. Riel surrendered. He was tried, sentenced to death for high treason, and, after two delays, was hanged in November 1885. The central government had taken a great deal of time to answer the Métis' petition about their land grants but took only a few months to send Riel to the gallows. Only six years after Riel's death the new, mainly English-speaking government of Manitoba virtually abolished the right of its French-speaking citizens to education in their mother tongue as well as their guaranteed right to use French in the province's courts and legislature.

Recently, more than 100 years after his death, the federal government officially pardoned Louis Riel. The sad story of this authentic French-Canadian hero, who opposed the oppression of his people by an anglophone majority in a doomed attempt to defend their language and culture, gives insight into some of the concerns of French-speaking Canadians.

IMMIGRATION

The first European immigrants came to the shores of Quebec by boat. They sailed up the St. Lawrence and from 1840 onward their first steps on Canadian soil were taken at Big Island–**Grosse-Île,** the quarantine island in the river not far from Quebec City. Thousands of Irish who left their homeland as a result of the potato famine in the 1840's are buried on this island. Many Irish orphans were adopted by Quebec families. It may come as a surprise that many Quebecers have English, Scottish and Irish surnames but may not even speak the English language.

From 1851 to 1911 three million people immigrated to Canada. Another three million came between the two Great Wars, and five million have come since World War II. They are from all nations and all walks of life, and many of them have chosen Quebec as their home.

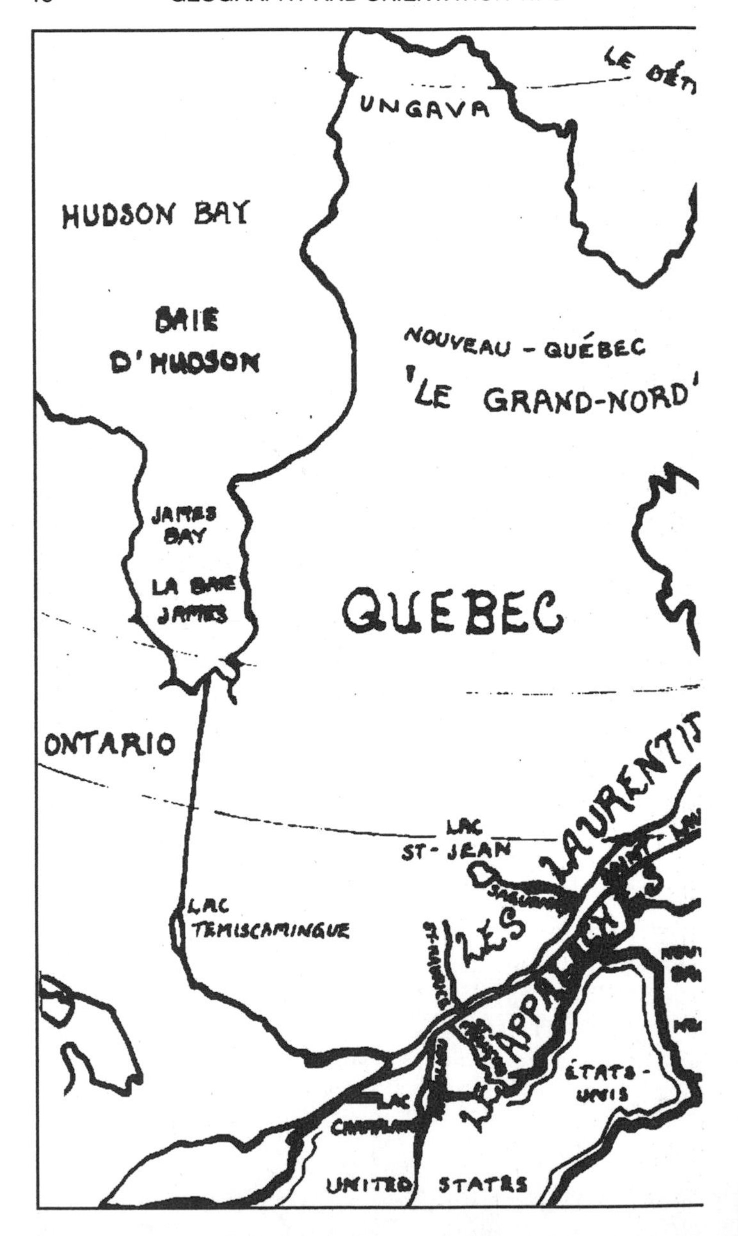
UNGAVA
HUDSON BAY
BAIE D'HUDSON
NOUVEAU - QUÉBEC
'LE GRAND-NORD'
JAMES BAY
LA BAIE JAMES
QUEBEC
ONTARIO
LAC ST-JEAN
LAC TEMISCAMINGUE
ÉTATS-UNIS
UNITED STATES

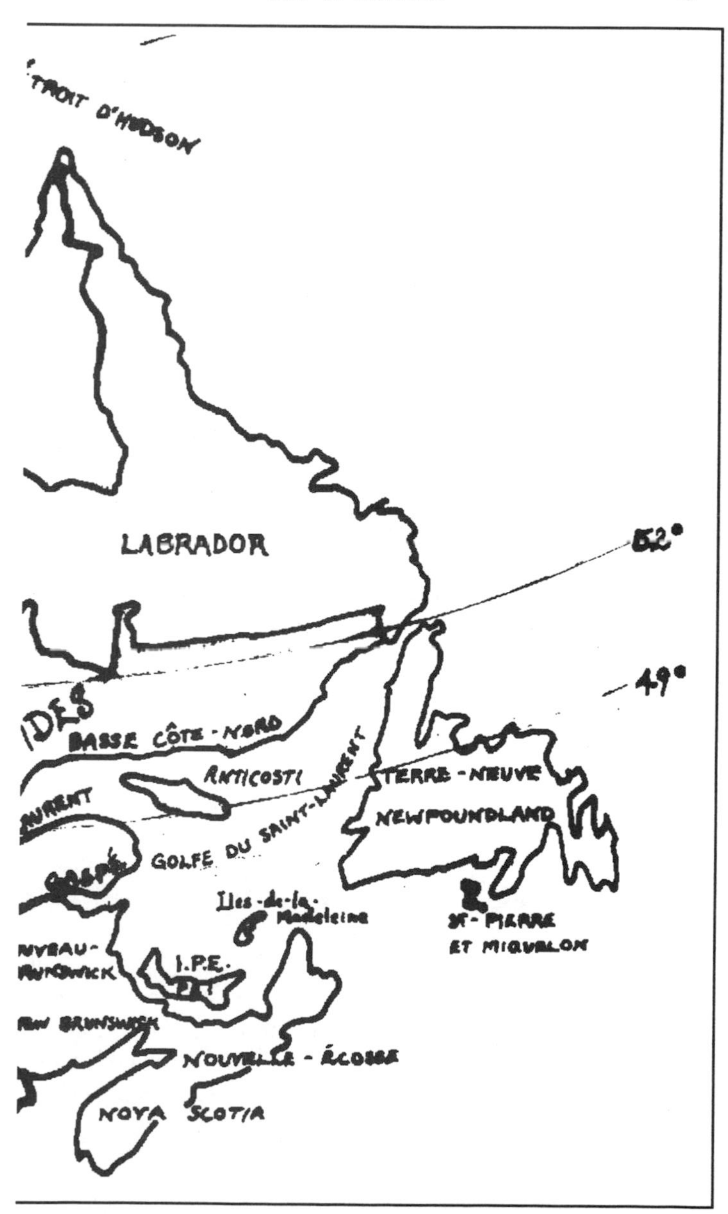
LABRADOR
52°
49°
BASSE CÔTE-NORD
ANTICOSTI
GOLFE DU SAINT-LAURENT
GASPÉ
TERRE-NEUVE
NEWFOUNDLAND
Iles-de-la-Madeleine
ST-PIERRE
ET MIQUELON
I.P.E.
NOUVELLE-ÉCOSSE
NOVA SCOTIA

CHAPTER 2

SOME QUEBEC GEOGRAPHY & ORIENTATION TIPS

It has been said about Canada that it has too little history and too much geography. Quebec has plenty of both.

FOLLOW THAT RIVER

Quebec is one vast piece of real estate stretching north nearly 2000 kilometers (1240 miles) from the northern United States (U.S.)–**les États-Unis (É.-U.)** to the Hudson Strait–**le détroit d'Hudson.** Its population is concentrated near the American borders of New York, Vermont, New Hampshire and Maine, and along the St. Lawrence River, with only sparse settlements north of the 49th parallel.

The St. Lawrence River–**le fleuve St-Laurent** runs from the southwest corner of the province at the Ontario border in a northeasterly direction, a distance of 1000 kilometers (600 miles). The river's gulf–**le Golfe du St-Laurent** is circled by the Gaspé Peninsula–**la Gaspésie,** Quebec's Lower North Shore–**la Basse-Côte-Nord,** and the four most easterly provinces of Canada: Newfoundland (Nfld.)–**la Terre-Neuve (T.-N.),** Nova Scotia (N.S.)–**la Nouvelle-Écosse (N.-É.),** Prince Edward Island (P.E.I.)–**l'Île du Prince-Édouard (Î.P.-É.),** New Brunswick (N.B.)–**le Nouveau-Brunswick (N.-B.).**

The relatively minuscule remains of New France that still belong to France, the islands of St-Pierre and Miquelon, nestle off the southwest tip of Newfoundland in **le Golfe.** The world-renowned hunting preserve of Anticosti Island–**l'Île d'Anticosti** and the Magdalen Islands–**les Îles-de-la-Madeleine,** famous for sand–**sable,** salt–**sel** and seals–**phoques,** are part of Quebec. They are situated in **le Golfe**.

The foothills of the Appalachian Mountains–**les Appalaches** are south of **le fleuve St-Laurent** and roughly parallel to it. The Canadian Shield–**le Bouclier canadien** and the Laurentian chain of mountains–**les Laurentides** highlight the topography of the region immediately north of **le fleuve.**

THE FAR NORTH–LE GRAND-NORD

Nearly half of Quebec is in the region designated for tourist purposes as the Far North–**le Grand-Nord.** Consider this: the northern tip of the Ungava Peninsula extends beyond the 62nd parallel, **le Grand-Nord** region begins at the 52nd. The American border–**la frontière des États-Unis** at New York, Vermont and New Hampshire is at the 45th parallel. That means there's a lot of land, accessible only by plane, inhabited by very few people, most of whom are members of the First Nations: the Cree, Inuit and Naskapi. These people usually have English as their first or second language.

As southern "comforts" have come to the North, so too has an entrepreneurial spirit. The native people and others are developing exciting Arctic adventures for those who want to explore their unique way of life. In winter, the land is a vast expanse of ice and snow. In the short explosive summer you can see the midnight sun.

Whatever the season, extensive preparations for excursions to **le Grand-Nord,** also called New Quebec–**Nouveau-Québec** are necessary. **Tourisme-Québec** can supply you with the information needed. There is a toll-free number for use in Canada and the United States: 1-800-363-7777.

HISTORIC TRAVEL ROUTES

The early highways on this continent were the rivers and lakes, and people travelled by canoe and other forms of water navigation. It's not surprising then that settlement patterns were near the various waterways.

The first major roadway, the King's Highway–**le chemin du Roy,** dates back to 1730. Now known as Route 138, it follows the north shore of the river–**le St-Laurent** in a primarily east-west direction and is definitely not an expressway. It is a wonderful scenic route through old villages and towns. The part of it that crosses the mouth of the Saguenay River is actually an efficient ferry for which there is no charge.

In the 1500s, there were three principal settlements on **le St-Laurent.** The Iroquois knew the present-day Quebec City as Stadacona,

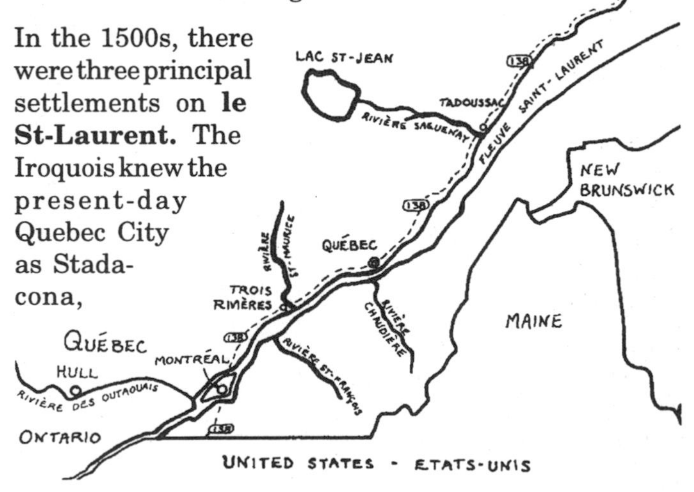

and Montreal as Hochelaga. Hochelaga was later christened Ville-Marie by the Jesuits and subsequently became **Mont Royal**–Montreal in honor of the King of France. Champlain used Kebec for **la ville de Québec** from an Algonquin word meaning "where the river narrows", which is precisely what **le St-Laurent** does near this provincial capital. Downstream from Quebec at the mouth of the Saguenay River was the largest fur-trading post on the continent—Tadoussac.

Three Rivers–**Trois-Rivières,** founded in 1634, was named after the three channels of the St. Maurice River in its harbor. Trois-Rivières is midway between Montreal and Quebec City on Highway 138 and **le St-Laurent.**

Note that in French there are words to distinguish between relative sizes of rivers. A very large river running into the ocean is **un fleuve,** a smaller one running into a lake or another river is **une rivière,** and a brook is **un ruisseau.** It might be useful to know that a stream is **un cours d'eau** and a riverbank is **une rive.**

WHERE MOST QUÉBÉCOIS LIVE

There are 7 million residents in Quebec with close to 500,000 in the Quebec City region, 200,000 in the Hull–Gatineau region, 160,000 in Chicoutimi–Jonquière, 140,000 in Sherbrooke and region, and 136,000 in the area around Trois-Rivières. The most densely populated areas of Quebec are along **le St-Laurent** and south of it. There are two major islands in **le fleuve,** and these islands are home to two of the largest cities in Quebec, Montreal (population about 1.9 million) and Laval (population approximately 350,000). The islands are separated by **la rivière des Prairies.**

WHERE QUEBEC'S ENGLISH-SPEAKING PEOPLE LIVE

An English-speaking person, perhaps apprehensive about his or her French-language skills, might consider visiting Quebec in stages or **étapes.** On the first visit, you might prefer to come to areas of the province where there is a significant English presence; then, once comfortable with the language and the customs, explore the rest of **la belle province.**

There are over 800,000 Quebecers who claim English as their mother tongue. Well over 70 per cent of them (more than half a million) live mainly in the western part of the urban area around Montreal and Laval. Both islands are accessed by bridges and a tunnel. You will have plenty to see and do in any season if you visit these island communities. The rest of the English-speaking community is widely dispersed, but the tourist regions of Mainland Quebec where you will find a fair concentration of anglophones are shown on the map below.

From west to east you see the Ottawa Valley–**l'Outaouais,** the Laurentians–**les Laurentides, Lanaudière, la Montérégie,** the Eastern Townships–**les**

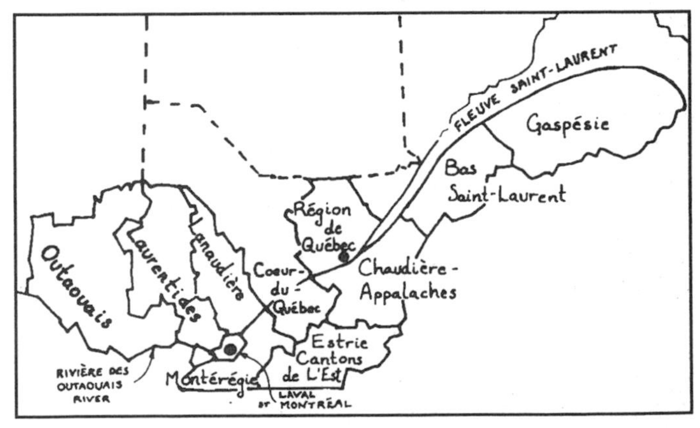

cantons de l'Est or **l'Estrie,** and Gaspé–**la Gaspésie.** In the region of the city of Quebec–**la Région de la ville de Québec** there are many bilingual **Québécois.**

SOME TRAVEL TIPS

Even-numbered routes go east to west more or less. (Memory hook: Even–East.) The mountains, rivers and lakes of this land make a straight grid for roads impossible. Roads with numbers under 100 are expressways–**les autoroutes;** those ending in zero respect the Even–East rule, and those ending in 5 are oriented mostly north–south. In Quebec, as a general rule, any road identified by three digits is a two-lane highway. Highway 20 is an expressway which at the Ontario border becomes Highway 401, an Ontario four-lane highway leading west to Kingston and Toronto.

We have mentioned the two island cities and access to them. Remember, too, that because of the Quebec climate, 90 per cent of road and bridge work takes place during the three months of summer when 75 per cent of our tourists are here and Quebec construction workers take a two-week vacation (the last two full weeks of July)! Don't be alarmed if you run into torn-up pavement, gaping holes, and partially constructed bridges. It all gets done before the next election.

To avoid the hassle, you may consider a visit to the off-island regions of the province where roads rarely get repaired. There are lots of wonderful things to enjoy and visit in Mainland Quebec—half a million square kilometers (200,000 square miles) waiting to be explored.

TOURIST REGION OF MONTREAL

Montreal, a wonderfully cosmopolitan city with a regional population of 1.9 million, is an island–**une île** accessible by numerous bridges and expressways. On weekday mornings and afternoons, radio stations devote whole programs to advising motorists how to get in and out of the city. The Montreal Urban Community (MUC)—**la Communauté urbaine de Montréal (CUM)** comprises 28 municipalities on the island and is the regional governing body.

It is strongly recommended that you use public transit or go on foot wearing comfortable walking shoes to visit the city centre, especially Old Montreal–**le Vieux Montréal,** the site of the greatest concentration of 17th, 18th and 19th century buildings in North America. Narrow cobblestone streets, outdoor plazas, restaurants, gift shops, and a museum of archaeology and history, **le musée de la Pointe-à-Callière,** make a trip to this section of town a "must". The recently restored Old Port–**le Vieux Port** is home to theatres, concerts, bicycle paths, and countless activities.

Follow the river and not the sun if you are trying to orient yourself in the vicinity of the island of Montreal. Pretend that **le fleuve St-Laurent** flows, as the roads department's signs claim, in a straight line on an east-west axis, and then the road signs will make sense. The Laurentians are considered to be north–**nord** of Montreal, and the south shore to be south–**sud.** The West Island of Montreal, where the population is mainly English-speaking, is actually west–**ouest** (and a little south). If you have a car compass, ignore it—and don't worry about the sun setting in the north.

Le fleuve widens just west of the Lachine Rapids–**les rapides** to form Lake St. Louis–**Lac St-Louis**, with historic sites dotting its shores. One street in Montreal, **la rue St-Laurent** (also called The Main), is considered to divide Montreal into east–**est** and west–**ouest.** So if you are looking for an address on Sherbrooke St. E.

don't start looking until you are east of **rue St-Laurent.**

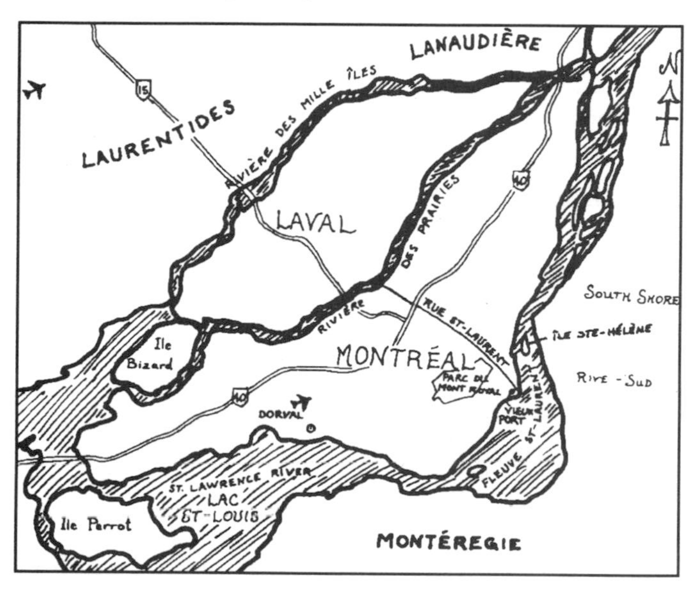

If you visit Montreal when the weather is inclement, use the snowy or wet days to explore our underground city–**la ville souterrain.** Twenty-nine kilometers of warm, dry passages, tied together by a modern subway system–**le Métro** connect a weather-free world. You can reach 1700 commercial businesses, 1600 boutiques, seven major hotels, three universities and three department stores. You'll find 45 bank branches, 34 cinemas, two exhibition halls, two railroad stations, the intercity bus terminal, the Olympic Stadium and many exciting restaurants. There are reports that a modern cave-dweller spent six months living in this maze without surfacing.

Walking in downtown Montreal–**Montréal centre-ville** above ground at night is quite safe. On warm spring and summer evenings you will encounter hordes of pedestrians on these streets–**les rues suivantes:** Ste-Catherine, St-Denis, La Gauchetière (in Chinatown), Crescent, and all areas of **le Vieux Montréal.**

There are countless other attractions in the city, just a few of which are the Botanical Gardens–**le Jardin botanique,** museums–**les musées** (like the Montreal Museum of Fine Arts–**le Musée des beaux-arts de Montréal),** St. Helen's Island–**Île Ste-Hélène,** the Casino–**le Casino,** the Biodome–**le Biodôme** (a living museum with several different ecosystems), and Montreal's crown jewel, the 200-hectare (500-acre) Mount Royal Park–**Parc du Mont-Royal.** The archives center–**les Archives nationales du Québec, Centre de Montréal** may be on your itinerary if you wish to trace your Quebec ancestors.

And don't forget the festivals: the International Jazz Festival–**Festival international de Jazz de Montréal** at the beginning of July, with indoor and outdoor concerts, many of them free; the Just for Laughs Festival–**Festival juste pour rire** at the end of July; the International Fireworks Competition–**le Concours international d'art pyrotechnique (feux d'artifice)** throughout the summer, and so on.

LAVAL

Northwest of the Island of Montreal and only minutes away by car is the second largest city in Quebec, the island city of Laval, created in 1965 by the amalgamation of 14 municipalities on **Île Jésus.** Laval is a modern city of over 350,000 residents, only a bridge away from the island of Montreal. **La rivière des Prairies** on the south of Laval separates it from Montreal, and **la rivière des Mille Îles,** the river of a thousand islands, separates it from the Laurentians–**les Laurentides.**

Laval is home to high-tech industries–**des industries de haute technologie,** large shopping and convention centres, some very productive farmland and some interesting historic sites, notably at Sainte-Rose, St-Vincent-de-Paul and St-François-de-Sales. It is also home to the Cosmodome and to the Space Science Centre and the Space Camp–**le Cosmodôme et le Centre de sciences de l'espace et le Camp spatial.**

FALLING IN LOVE WITH QUEBEC

Quebec has a lot to offer: history, a rich cultural and architectural heritage, a landmass with interesting topography and a wide diversity of flora and fauna. It also boasts modern technology, a population of seven million people a third of whom can converse in both English and French with ease, an unparalleled opportunity to use a foreign language, and a European experience here in North America. Add to this an extensive road network and an incredible range of climate, and you have a fascinating place to visit or live.

CHAPTER 3

MAINLAND QUEBEC–WHAT TO SEE AND DO

The Quebec Ministry of Tourism has divided **la province de Québec** into 19 tourist regions, and each Regional Tourist Association–**Association Touristique Régionale (A.T.R.)** publishes a tourist guide booklet in both English and French versions. All guides are identical in size and format, with the year of the edition in the upper right hand corner.

These booklets are usually updated every year, and they are chock full of information, some history, some publicity, hotel and motel information, activities, and so on. Since the format is common to all regions, once you are accustomed to the layout you will find them extremely helpful. We highly recommend that you pick up these guides, which are free of charge–**gratuites, gratis** or **sans frais.** However, the official route map of Quebec will cost you $2.50 plus taxes—but this is the best road map of the province. Call **Tourisme-Québec** at 1-800-363-7777 for information, guides and map.

Montreal and Laval, the two island cities introduced in Chapter 2, are home to over two million of Quebec's seven million inhabitants.

Visiting the Far North–**le Grand-Nord** requires special preparations.

Here follows a thumbnail sketch of Quebec's other tourist regions. The regions of Mainland Quebec are laid out starting at the west. Those regions where there is a considerable English presence are described first. At the end of this book there is a fold-out map which shows the location of the tourist regions.

THE OTTAWA VALLEY–L'OUTAOUAIS

Just off the west end of **l'île de Montréal, la rivière des Outaouais** (oo-tah-weh), named after the **Outaouais** or Ottawa tribe, joins **le fleuve St-Laurent.** If you follow the river 100 kilometers (60 miles) due west you will come to Hull, which, with Ottawa in Ontario, forms part of the National Capital Region of Canada. The region north of Hull, like the river, is called **l'Outaouais.** Many federal civil servants live in this region, and there is a large bilingual and English-speaking population.

L'Outaouais is reputed to have been a source of timber for the ships of the British Navy that fought during the Napoleonic Wars, and forestry and pulp and paper industries still dominate the region. In Hull, the Canadian museum of civilizations–**le Musée canadien des civilisations** stands on the banks of the river and is well worth a visit.

North of Hull is **le parc de la Gatineau,** which, for the politically aware, includes the famed Meech Lake. It is also a great outdoor recreation area. **La rivière Gatineau** has its source far to the north of the park, and the forestry town of Maniwaki is one of the larger service areas near the nature reserve, **la réserve faunique de La Vérendrye,** where hunting and fishing reign. In this region **la rivière des Outaouais** is the border between Ontario and Quebec. Upriver from Hull is the mainly English-speaking region of Pontiac. Downriver is Montebello, where the hotel Château Montebello stands, believed to be the world's largest log structure.

THE LAURENTIANS–LES LAURENTIDES

Just east of **l'Outaouais** is the Laurentian region–**les Laurentides.** Easily accessible from Montreal, this is cottage country–**un centre de villégiature** and also great terrain for downhill skiing–**le ski alpin.** Montrealers often escape the city to go "up north", which is as much west as north of the city. The region **les Laurentides** has three distinct sections—the St. Lawrence Lowlands, or Lower Laurentians, the Central Laurentians where most of the downhill skiing is found, and the Upper Laurentians, marked by forests, nature reserves, and rugged countryside.

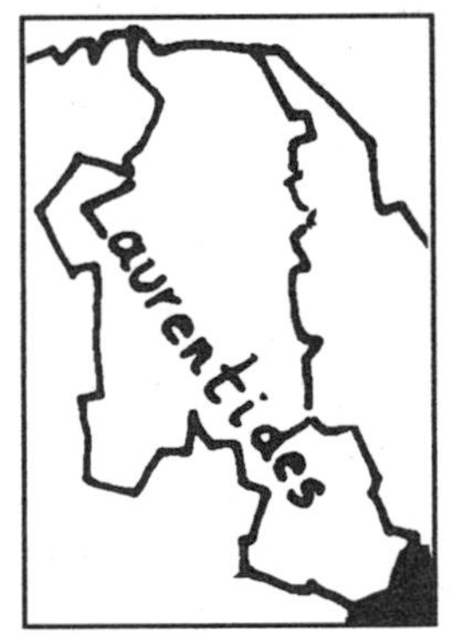

The Lower Laurentians–**les Basses Laurentides** region is flat with good farmland. You will also find high-tech industries, such as General Motors and Bell Helicopter, and a rich architectural heritage. St-Eustache, Lachute and St-Jerome have many heritage sites. The Central Laurentians country features downhill skiing both night and day, fine dining, theatres and tourist towns like Ste-Adèle, Ste-Agathe and St-Sauveur. Mont Tremblant is a Laurentian village and world-renowned resort at the northern end of the Central Laurentians.

The North River–**la rivière du Nord** cuts through the Laurentian Shield for a distance of over 330 km (200 mi.) The Red River–**la rivière Rouge** has become famous for its white-water rafting, particularly exciting when the water is high in the spring or after heavy summer rains.

LANAUDIÈRE

Immediately east of **les Laurentides** is **Lanaudière,** stretching from the plains–**les plaines du fleuve St-Laurent** to the Laurentian foothills–**le piedmont des Laurentides** and the Laurentian plateau–**le plateau Laurentien.** From 1637 on, **seigneuries** were established along **le fleuve** by the newly arrived colonists–**les colons** from France. The vestiges of some of these properties can be found along Highway 138, **le chemin du Roy,** which dates back to 1730 and runs along **le fleuve St-Laurent** at the south end of this region.

In the southern section of **Lanaudière,** cities like Terrebonne and Mascouche are suburbs–**des banlieues** of Montreal. Several years ago, a rich musical tradition led to the establishment of an international classical music festival, **le Festival international de Lanaudière,** which is still a huge attraction. Concerts take place in the outdoor amphitheatre or in any of a number of churches in the area around Joliette from the end of June until mid-August.

Lanaudière is dotted with lakes and laced with rivers. There are excellent facilities for outdoor recreation both summer and winter. It is only a short drive from Montreal.

LA MONTÉRÉGIE

South of **le St-Laurent** and Montreal lie the valleys of the Chateauguay and Richelieu Rivers in the tourist region of **la Montérégie,** relatively flat land with much good farmland. It is also mighty fine apple country. The section of **la Montérégie** adjacent to the Ontario border features an outdoor recreation area around Mont Rigaud as well as some of Quebec's finest equestrian centers–**des centres équestres.** In July, the Speedboat Regatta at Valleyfield draws spectators from far and wide.

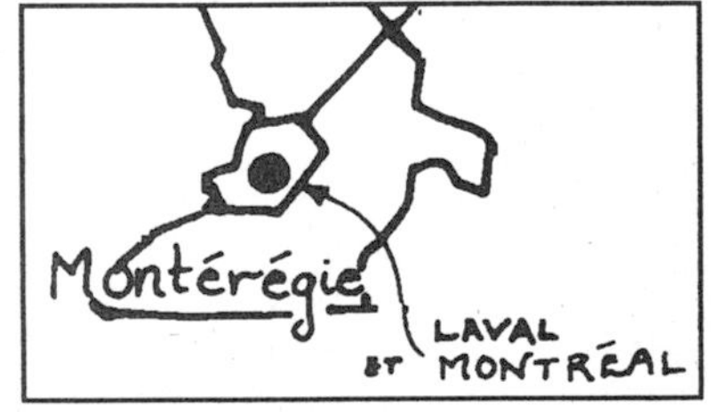

The Indian Reserve of Kahnawake and the city of Châteauguay are just across the Mercier Bridge–**le pont Mercier** from **l'île de Montréal.** Nearby on **la rivière Châteauguay** near Allan's Corners is the site of a battle of the War of 1812 where the British forces led by Lt. Col. de Salaberry held off an American force trying to invade Canada.

La rivière Richelieu, which flows into **le fleuve St-Laurent** at Sorel, was the site of much activity during the Rebellion of **les Patriotes** in 1837. Along the Richelieu there are heritage sites including Fort Chambly, Fort Lennox and St-Jean-sur-Richelieu.

The most densely populated section of **la Montérégie** is the South Shore–**la Rive-Sud,** which, if you consult a map, you will note is mostly due east of **l'île de Montréal,** rather than south as you would expect from its name. **Le fleuve St-Laurent** refuses to flow east-west, and this is why Longueuil, St-Lambert, Varennes and Verchères are found east of Montreal on **la Rive-Sud.**

THE EASTERN TOWNSHIPS–LES CANTONS DE L'EST

East of **la Montérégie** is the area best known as the Eastern Townships–**les Cantons de l'Est** or **l'Estrie.** Both terms are used in French. **L'Estrie** is the administrative district which surrounds the Sherbrooke area, while **les Cantons de l'Est** is a historic region which extends as far west as the Richelieu River.

Both **la Montérégie** and **les Cantons de l'Est** have substantial English-speaking populations. The 13,000 square kilometers (5000 sq. mi.) of the "Townships" include mountains, rolling farmland and lush valleys. Lakes Memphremagog, Massawippi and Megantic were named by the Abenaki Indians, the first settlers in the region. After the American War of Independence in 1776 they were joined by Loyalists ("Tories" to the Americans), those who remained loyal to the British crown and left the colonies to the south. Many of the villages near the American border–**la frontière américaine** have architecture which resembles that of the villages of New England–**la Nouvelle-Angleterre.**

The tourist region of the Eastern Townships starts at Lake Champlain and extends some 300 kilometers (185 miles) east to the Maine border. Major ski hills (Bromont, Sutton, Orford and Owl's Head) dominate the central section, and Granby, Cowansville, Magog and Sherbrooke are busy industrial and commercial areas.

The Townships is cottage country–**un centre de villégiature** for thousands of city residents. It is well endowed with lakes and other outdoor recreational facilities. The Piggery Summer Theatre in North Hatley and the Brome Lake Theatre in Knowlton, part of **la ville de**

Lac-Brome, have English productions. French summer theatres–**des théâtres d'été** abound.

Bishop's University, founded in 1843, still receives both English and French-speaking students in Lennoxville near Sherbrooke. Nearby is **l'Université de Sherbrooke,** which among its many courses offers a well respected English writing course. The place-names of the region are indicative of its colonization by English-speaking settlers.

GASPÉ–LA GASPÉSIE

The eastern tip of Quebec which reaches out into **le golfe du St-Laurent** has been a tourist mecca ever since the well-to-do built cottages in the 1800s in places like Métis Beach, Percé and Carleton. **La Gaspésie,** a peninsula 280 kilometers (175 miles) long and 144 km. (90 miles) wide, offers amazing scenery along its 900 km (560 mi.) coastline. The seafood is exceptional in this part of the world and the inhabitants are very friendly. Many of them are English-speaking. Here parks and wildlife reserves–**des réserves fauniques** proliferate.

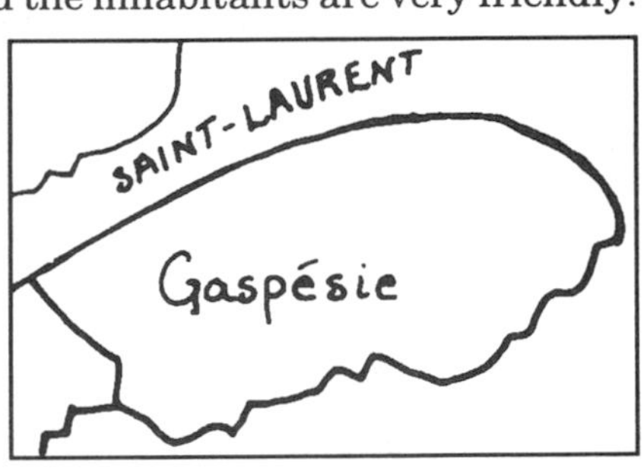

One unique spot on the coast is the former summer estate of Lord Mount Stephen, the first president of the Canadian Pacific Railway. His niece Elsie Stephen Meighen Reford transformed the estate, perched on the shore at Grand-Métis, into a botanical wonderland. **Les Jardins de Métis** boast of hundreds of native and exotic species and varieties of plants, trees and shrubs.

Major population centers are Matane, Ste-Anne-des-Monts, Gaspé, Percé, and New Richmond. The Chic-Choc Mountains, also called **les Monts Notre-Dame,** the very end of the Appalachians–**les Appalaches,** are found in **la Gaspésie.** The tip of the peninsula is the national (federal) park **Parc national Forillon,** which features hiking trails, camping facilities, historic buildings and more. Gaspé village, the region's administrative center, overlooks a sheltered harbor into which flow three salmon rivers. A winding scenic road from Gaspé 120 kilometers (75 miles) long leads to the village of Percé with its sensational rock **le Rocher Percé,** accessible by foot at low tide. A short boat ride from the town takes you to the bird sanctuary at **Parc de l'Île Bonaventure.**

The south shore of the peninsula and the north shore of New Brunswick sandwich **la Baie-des-Chalcurs.** Former Quebec premier René Levesque's home is in New Carlisle, but he was born in a hospital across the bay in Campbellton, New Brunswick. **Chaleurs** means heat, warmth, warm weather, and **la Baie-des-Chaleurs** is relatively warm. On the shores of the bay a British historic village can be found at New Richmond. The neighboring village of Carleton, named after Sir Guy Carleton, is best known for windsurfing; and a world-famous fish and plant fossil museum is sited in the nearby **Parc de Miguasha. Les rivières Matapédia, Cascapédia** and **Restigouche** are all renowned for their salmon fishing. The Micmac Indians have reserves at Maria and Restigouche.

QUEBEC CITY REGION

Downriver from Montreal is the capital city of Quebec–**la ville de Québec,** North America's only fortified city and a world heritage site. A scant two percent of the population of this region uses English as its first language, but thousands of tourists visit the region, and service is usually available in English as well as French. There is much to see and do in the city: fabulous dining, outdoor cafés, street musicians, and museums. Throughout the world the Winter Carnival–**le Carnaval de Québec** is known with its mascot **Bonhomme Carnaval** (the oversized snowman with his colorful **ceinture fléchée,** a long multi-colored woven belt).

Accessible from Quebec City by car–**par auto** or by bicycle–**par vélo** is Montmorency Falls–**la chute Montmorency,** impressive in summer, extraordinary in winter. The Island of Orleans–**l'Île d'Orléans** is a pastoral haven also close to the city and the falls; it is embellished by French-Canadian architecture.

A short drive from the city on the north shore of **le St-Laurent** is the basilica–**la basilique de Sainte-Anne-de-Beaupré,** and not far from it is **le parc du Mont-Sainte-Anne,** where downhill skiing is king. The national (federal) wildlife reserve at Cap-Tourmente–**la réserve nationale de faune du Cap-Tourmente,** 50 kilometers (30 miles) downriver from Quebec, is an exceptional area for migrating wildfowl.

The King's Highway–**le chemin du Roy,** Route 138, heads west from Quebec City through several historic villages. To the north of the city, rugged countryside, panoramic views, rushing rivers, many lakes and mountains, and **le parc de la Jacques-Cartier** allow for all the recreation activities the most enthusiastic outdoors person could want.

CHAUDIÈRE–APPALACHES

South of **le fleuve** and northeast of the Eastern Townships is the tourist region named **Chaudière-Appalaches.** It is dominated by **la rivière Chaudière,** notorious for its ice jams and spring flooding. You also find the Thetford Mines area, known for mining asbestos–**l'amiante,** and the region known as **la Beauce** with its rolling hills, maple bushes, snowmobile trails and **les Beaucerons. Les Beaucerons** are the local residents; they speak French in amazingly fast spurts and exhibit a fiercely entrepreneurial spirit.

Chaudière-Appalaches also includes the shore of **le fleuve St-Laurent** south of **la ville de Québec** where some of the first settlers farmed and built sawmills–**les moulins à scie** and grist mills–**les moulins à blé** or **farine.** The architectural richness of some of the villages such as Lotbinière, Lévis, Beaumont, Montmagny and St-Roch-des-Aulnaies is worth exploring.

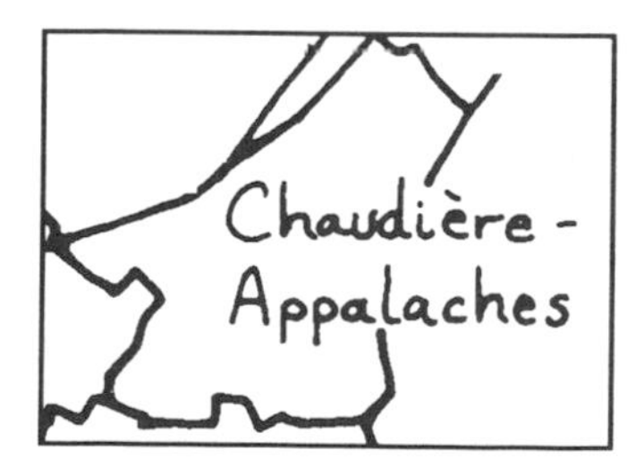

Grosse-Île, the quarantine island, is a National (federal) Historic Site. It can be reached by boat from the town of Berthier-sur-mer (**sur mer** means by the sea) just west of Montmagny. Montmagny is one of the older settlements in this area and is the site of the snow goose festival–**le Festival de l'oie blanche,** held to bid farewell to these graceful birds as they head south in October. A Maritime museum, **le musée maritime Bernier,** at l'Islet-sur-mer will give you an overview of the early history of the river.

THE LOWER ST LAWRENCE–LE BAS-ST-LAURENT

Le Bas-Saint-Laurent tourist region is the area bordered on the north by **le fleuve St-Laurent** and on the south by the state of Maine–**l'état du Maine** and the province of New Brunswick–**la province du Nouveau-Brunswick.** Lakes, rivers, peat bogs, distinctive architecture and controlled hunting areas–**des zones d'exploitation contrôlée (ZECs)** are found away from the river.

The principal population centers are Rivière-du-Loup and Rimouski, both of which are on the river–**sur le bord du fleuve.** At Rivière-du-Loup, **le fleuve** is some 23 kilometers (14 miles) wide and from here on is referred to as the sea–**la mer.** Along the shore of the river, from Kamouraska all the way to Sainte-Luce-sur-Mer, a distance of nearly 200 kilometers (125 miles), you can explore historic villages, visit areas first exploited by Basque fishermen, and meet some of those who make their living from the sea.

Regularly scheduled ferries–**les traversiers** leave for the north shore of the river from Rivière-du-Loup, Trois-Pistoles and Rimouski, should you want to combine a short trip on the river and explore both shores–**les deux rives du fleuve** on the same trip.

LA MAURICIE ET LES BOIS-FRANCS

The region known as the Heart of Quebec–**le Coeur-du-Québec** straddles **le fleuve St-Laurent** almost equidistant from Quebec, Montreal and Sherbrooke.

South of **le fleuve** is the hardwood forest area called **les Bois-francs,** famous for its furniture makers and, of course, for its maple syrup. The former residence of Sir Wilfrid Laurier, the first French-speaking prime minister of Canada, is now a museum in the town of Arthabaska. The industrial center of the area south of **le St-Laurent** is Drummondville, situated on **la rivière St-François.** Here in the warm weather of July, the world folklore festival–**le festival mondial de folklore** hosts singers and dancers at a giant outdoor party. Nearby is a village recreating the lifestyle in rural Quebec from 1810 to 1910, **le Village québécois d'Antan,** open only during warm weather.

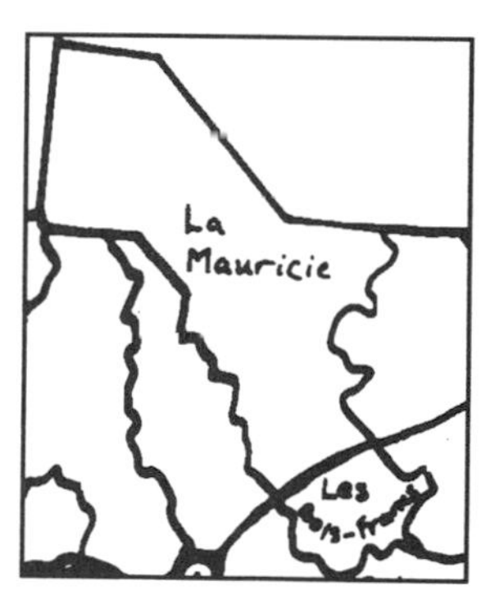

Le fleuve St-Laurent widens to form Lac St-Pierre, an excellent outdoor recreation area. The Abenaki village of Odanak is nearby. The north shore of **le fleuve** is renowned for its pulp and paper industries and for the dynamism of its principal city, **Trois-Rivières.** Another famous politician and premier of Quebec for many years, Maurice Duplessis, was a native of this city. **Le Vieux Trois-Rivières** (the city is over 350 years old) and the shrine **Sanctuaire Notre-Dame-du-Cap** at Cap-de-la-Madeleine are well worth exploring. A national (federal) historic site marking the first foundry in Canada, **le lieu historique national des Forges-du-Saint-Maurice,** sits on the banks of **la rivière St-Maurice** just north of Trois-Rivières.

La rivière St-Maurice gives its name to the region often referred to as **la Mauricie** north of **le St-Laurent.**

Le St-Maurice reaches far into the north of this region, passing by Shawinigan (birthplace of Canada's current prime minister Jean Chrétien) and La Tuque. Between Grand-Mère and La Tuque the federal government has established a national park with superb outdoor recreational facilities for camping, canoe-camping, and hiking, in **le parc national de la Mauricie.** The residents of **le Coeur-du-Québec** are primarily French-speaking, but at all federal parks and institutions you will find documentation and information in both English and French.

CHARLEVOIX

The farther you venture downriver (northeast), the more rugged and less populated is the territory. The Canadian Shield–**le Bouclier canadien** dominates the landscape. Charming villages dot the hillsides, and magnificent hotels welcome tourists in Charlevoix, long ago discovered by painters, poets, writers and musicians. The flora and fauna–**la flore et la faune** abouund in wide variety, and salt water and fresh water meet at the northern limit of this region. In 1988, UNESCO declared the region a World Biosphere Reserve–**une réserve mondiale de la Biosphère.** It is the first such reserve to be inhabited, and it is only 120 km (75 mi.) from **la ville de Québec.**

Cap-Tourmente, overlapping the Quebec city tourist region to the west and the marine park, **le Parc marin du Saguenay,** at Baie-Ste-Catherine to the east are attractions which show off the natural treasures of this part of Quebec.

Some of the memorable sites of Charlevoix include Le Massif, a downhill ski area; Baie Saint-Paul, an artists' haven; the island of the hazelnuts–**l'Île aux Coudres,** with vestiges from the past; and Murray Bay–**la Malbaie** and its hotel and casino **le Manoir Richelieu.**

MANICOUAGAN, DUPLESSIS AND THE NORTH SHORE

Adjacent to Charlevoix but still near **le St-Laurent,** we find the tourist area of Manicouagan with endless snowfields, ideal for snowmobile and dogsled expeditions. Here remains of fur trading posts and Basque fishing stops have been found along the riverbank.

One of the engineering feats for which Quebec is famous, the Manic-5 dam–**le barrage Manic-Cinq** produces immense amounts of electricity. It is located in this region near the town of Manicouagan. Here you can see the transition from boreal forest to tundra. Tadoussac and Baie-Comeau are two of the larger towns in Manicouagan.

Duplessis is the most easterly part of Quebec on the north shore of **le St-Laurent.** It is a mecca for hardy souls willing to experience temperature extremes to enjoy their favorite outdoor sports. Parts of Duplessis are accessible only by boat, including **l'Île d'Anticosti** and the national (federal) park, **Parc des Îles Mingan.**

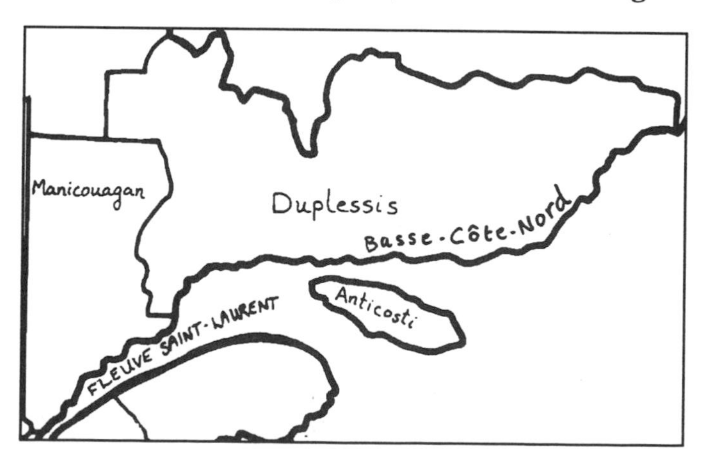

Seven Islands–**Sept-Îles** is an important port.

Manicouagan and Duplessis present nature at its most unspoiled. Both are known for whale watching and bird watching–**l'observation des baleines et des oiseaux,** controlled hunting and fishing zones–**les zones d'exploitation contrôlée (ZECs),** and outfitters–**les pourvoiries.**

Along the coast at the very end of Quebec across the Strait of Belle-Isle–**le détroit de Belle-Isle** from Newfoundland is the Lower North Shore–**la Basse-Côte-Nord.** In **La Basse-Côte-Nord** are a number of hamlets with French names but populated by many English-speaking people. The area is accessible by boat, plane or snowmobile—it has very few roads.

THE MAGDALEN ISLANDS–LES ÎLES-DE-LA-MADELEINE

The archipelago of **les Îles-de-la-Madeleine** is composed of about a dozen islands in the shape of a half moon in the Gulf–**le Golfe du St-Laurent.** Six of the islands are connected by a road across long thin sand dunes. The climate here is less rigorous than in the rest of the province, and the water surrounding the islands is warmer than along the banks of **le fleuve.** Winds are constant, and they sometimes play havoc with shipping. There are some 300 kilometers (200 miles) of sand beaches, and the region is a windsurfer's paradise.

At the southern tip of the archipelago there is the virtually treeless Entry Island–**l'Île d'Entrée,** population about 200 English-speaking souls, accessible by daily ferry from Cap-Aux-Meules on Grindstone Island –**l'Île du Cap-aux-Meules.** The most southerly island in the chain is **l'Île du Havre Aubert,** more populous, (2500 mostly French-speaking persons), having more forest and a road which can take you to **l'Île du Cap-aux-**

Meules, the business and administrative center of the archipelago. Spectacular cliffs and rock formations abound. The next island to the north is **l'Île du Havre-aux-Maisons,** the site of the airport–**l'aéroport** serving the island, and of some amazing sand dunes–**les dunes de sable** and lagoons–**les barachois.**

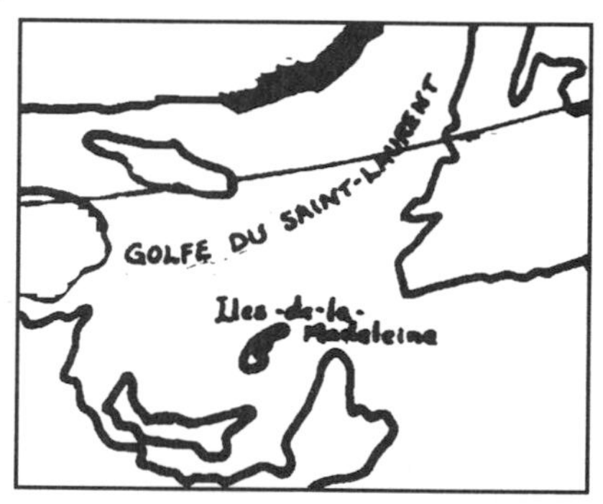

The Island of the Wolves–**l'Île-aux-Loups** and its only village, Pointe-aux-Loups, which has spectacular beaches on each side, are the clam–**palourdes** capital of the region. The last two islands are Big Island–**Grosse-Île** and Grand Entry Island–**l'Île de la Grande Entrée.**

Years ago the settlement of Old Harry on Grosse-Île was the site of walrus hunting. The walrusses would lie in the sun on Shipwreck Beach–**la plage de la grande Échouerie** and become victims of those hunting them for the oil in their fat.

Les Madelinots, as the islanders are called, live principally from fishing, and **Grande-Entrée** is the lobster–**homard** capital of the islands. The islands are accessible by plane–**par avion** and by ferry–**par traversier** from **la Gaspésie** and from Prince Edward Island–**l'Île-du-Prince-Édouard,** or by cargo boat from Montreal.

SAGUENAY–LAC-ST-JEAN

The residents of the **Lac Saint-Jean** area, nicknamed **les Bleuets** because of the abundance of blueberries there, are a hardy lot. They live in an extraordinarily beautiful part of Quebec. Like most Quebecers, **les Bleuets** enjoy partying. They have a great winter carnival in February–**le Carnaval souvenir de Chicoutimi,** and a **Festival des Bleuets** in Mistassini in August. In the summer, they also host an international swimming race across **Lac Saint-Jean.**

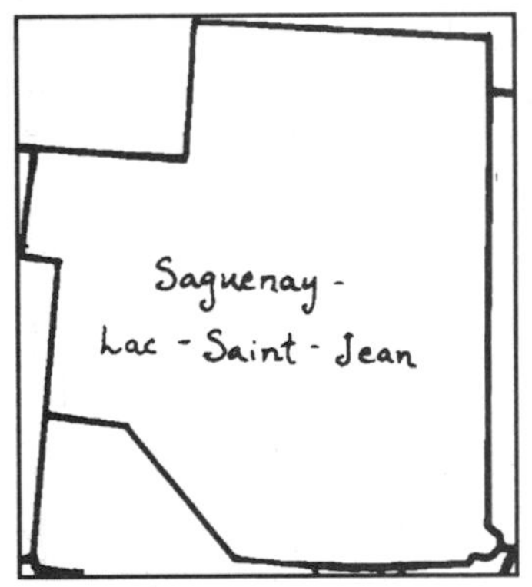

La rivière Saguenay leads from **Lac Saint-Jean** into **le fleuve St-Laurent** and features some of the most spectacular scenery in Quebec. You won't have to go to Scandinavia to say you have seen a fjord–**un fjord** (see—French isn't difficult) if you take a cruise on the Saguenay. **Le parc du Saguenay** is a protected area on both sides of the fjord, and the park is a hiker's dream.

The region is often referred to as the Kingdom of the Saguenay–**le Royaume du Saguenay,** and in La Baie more than 200 local residents stage a historical pageant in early summer called **La Fabuleuse Histoire d'un Royaume**–the fabulous history of a kingdom. They mount a second equally impressive **"spectacle"** called **Le Tour du Monde de Jos Maquillon** later in the summer.

There are 300,000 residents in the region, and it is well worth a visit. Many people are employed in the aluminum and pulp and paper industries. The Jonquière Junior College–**le CEGEP de Jonquière** has been giving

French immersion courses to diplomats, politicians and business executives for years. Most of the residents are French-speaking, but they will go to great lengths to make you feel at home.

ABITIBI–TÉMISCAMINGUE

Abitibi-Témiscamingue is a tourist region which covers 116,000 square kilometers (45,000 sq. mi.). The most northerly point is James Bay–**la Baie James.** If you are travelling by car, pay attention to the guide books. The highway–**la route de la Baie James** goes from Matagami to Radisson and on to the Hydro Electric complex at La Grande. It is 620 km (420 miles) long, and gas and emergency services are available at kilometer 381 (Mile 240). Imagine running out of gas on that road!

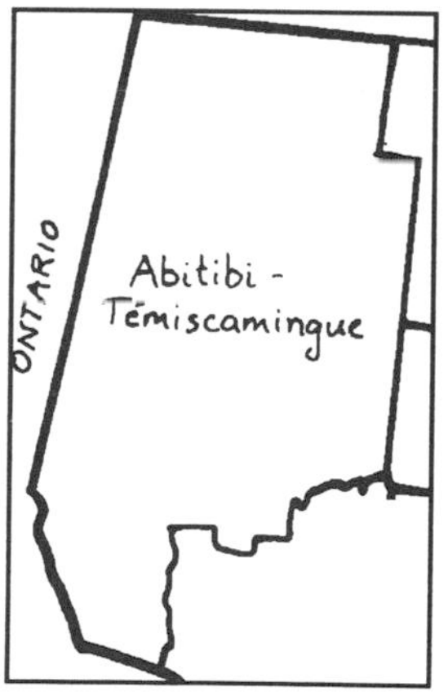

South of **la Baie James** is **l'Abitibi,** one of the richest regions for natural resources in Quebec. It is renowned for three minerals: gold–**l'or,** copper–**le cuivre,** and zinc–**le zinc,** and of course for its forests–**les forêts** and great hunting and fishing–**la chasse et la pêche.** Some of the noteworthy mining towns are Val d'Or, Malartic, and Rouyn-Noranda. Amos is an important forestry center situated on the second longest navigable river in Canada, **la rivière Harricana.** The Harricana River has given its name to an annual international snow-mobile race across northern Quebec.

South of the Abitibi region and next to the Ontario border, we find **Lac Témiscamingue,** around which there are many farm and forestry operations. It is possible to navigate from Notre-Dame-du-Nord across Lac Témiscamingue to the main town–**le chef-lieu** Ville-Marie (population 3,715), and down **la rivière des Outaouais** all the way to Pembroke in Ontario. **La rivière des Outaouais** forms the border between Ontario and Quebec, and the highway meanders from one side of the river to the other. The tourist regions of **Abitibi-Témiscamingue** and **l'Outaouais** share the territory of **la Réserve faunique La Vérendrye.**

Et voilà, la belle province!

CHAPTER 4

THE CLIMATE AND BEING PREPARED FOR IT

THE JOYS OF WINTER—L'HIVER, YES, SIR!

Have you ever been in a place where the temperature hit –40°? That's where the Fahrenheit and Celsius scales meet and Quebecers get together in parking lots for "un boost". The deep freeze usually strikes in January–**janvier** or early February–**février** and starts more conversations than cars.

An appreciation of the climate only adds to our admiration of the first builders in the old cities, Old Montreal–**le vieux Montréal** and Old Quebec–**le vieux Québec.** Early pioneers learned not to cut corners. The structures they built have withstood more than 300 years of varying temperatures. Even when building something as simple as a fence the builder had to ensure that its foundation was below the frost line–**la ligne de gel.** The average frost line in southern Quebec is at a depth of five feet (1.5 meters). However in certain cases it can be as deep as 8 or 9 feet (2 to 3 meters). And in northern Quebec they build on permafrost!

So if your host has installed his water pipe two feet below ground, he'll be chopping ice for water all winter. In the spring when the frost comes out of the ground it lifts rocks, clumps of dirt, buried tree stumps, and Bowser's bones. It's no kinder to Quebec highways. The snow-packed cracks of winter become spring craters to be patched by the local roads department–**la voirie.**

Over 250 cm (100 in.) of snow–**la neige** blankets much of southern Quebec each year. Thousands of workers with snow removal equipment effectively keep the roads clear of the white stuff. Even in rural areas, most of the secondary and even the gravel roads are cleared within hours of a snow storm–**une tempête de neige.**

The first dustings of snow come in November–**novembre,** and that's when out-of-practice Quebec drivers tend to slip and slide on hilly terrain. Most cars are equipped with snow tires–**les pneus d'hiver** or **de neige,** which are usually removed in spring. You won't want to venture too far into the countryside without at least all-season tires–**les pneus quatre saisons.** Driving is tricky when snow or freezing rain is falling, but is quite ordinary on a dry sunny day.

La ville de Québec and most of Eastern Quebec receive a thicker blanket of snow than Montreal. In winter the cities sprout thousands of plastic tents in driveways. These temporary garages–**ces garages temporaires** are as close to the road as the law permits to get their owners out of shovelling tons of snow over the winter. The winter of 1995 saw modern technology help one temporary garage owner. Heavy snow caused it to collapse on him, but he had a cellular phone in his pocket and was able to call for aid.

HELPING THE FAMILY CAR THROUGH THE COLD

The wide variation in temperature is hard on cars, and there are some routines Quebecers use to keep vehicles functioning even in the coldest weather. Most cars have little umbilical cords hanging out at the front with a plug on the end. This is to allow the engine block–**"le**

bloc" to be attached to an electrical outlet so that the block heater–**la chauffe-moteur** or **le bloc heater** will keep the engine warm and the car will start. If a car with a weak battery doesn't have one, it may need a "boost"–**un boost.** Booster cables–**des câbles** connect the battery of a car that is running to the "dead" battery, giving it a "boost" to get it started. A warning: boosting a car should be done by a knowledgeable person.

In January–**janvier** and February–**février,** you may see folks with cardboard or fancy covers attached to the front grill of the car. These act as windbreaks, allowing the heat produced by the car's engine to stay in the engine and get to the passenger compartment. By the way, assume your car will be dirty most of the winter. It's better not to go through a car wash unless the temperature is above freezing. Otherwise you may have the joyful experience of climbing into your car through the trunk because the doors and windows have frozen shut.

WINTER IS A CHALLENGE BUT FUN TOO!

Cold nights are great for cuddling, for chatting and for wild dancing—which you can find in discos and other night spots. Even November–**novembre** can be quite delightful, with lovely warm days (10°C) and clear crisp nights. There may be some rain–**la pluie,** freezing rain–**le verglas,** or light snow–**des flocons de neige.** Many tourist facilities, especially in outlying areas, close in **novembre** and early December–**décembre.** In the cities, museums, cultural events and concerts are the choice activities during these months.

From **décembre** through March–**mars** snow accumulates and people engage in outdoor sports activities. There may be the odd day of rain during this period, but downhill ski centers rarely suffer for lack of snow, most being equipped with state-of-the-art snow-making equipment. Cross-country skiing is more likely to be affected by rain, especially in the more southerly areas. Snowmobile rides, ice fishing and other activities don't miss a beat because of rain.

When southern Quebec is chilly, you can imagine how cold it is farther north. The combination of cold temperatures and high winds is a challenge to be confronted seriously. The hardy souls who live in the Far North all year round consider the cold no more than a nuisance. Adapting to the cold is a matter of being prepared for it.

Every two or three years, a severe blizzard will hit southern Quebec and dump anything from 40 to 100 cm. (a foot and a half to 3 feet) of snow on parts of the province. The weather forecast–**la météo** will have been issuing weather advisories, and an exciting calm will descend before the storm. Don't try to drive—stay indoors, and after the storm dies down, take a walk in the snow. After a fresh snowfall, sounds are muffled and snowflakes sparkle like diamonds in the light. Return to sit by a cosy fire and enjoy a fine meal, a good book or a lively conversation.

Every school board plans for at least 3 or 4 "snow days" a year—when the schools will close because of the weather. There are very few days in the year when driving is a real risk. Often an unsalted or unsanded driveway is more hazardous than the well maintained highways. Just as there is zero traction on a wet ice cube, there is zero traction on an icy road or driveway covered with a thin layer of water.

FINALLY, SPRING–ENFIN, LE PRINTEMPS!

By the end of **février, les Québécois** are ready to welcome the first warm days of spring, spring skiing on corn snow, and "sugaring off" parties–**le temps des sucres.** The sap–**la sève** begins to rise in the maples when days are sunny and mild and well above 0°C (32°F), and nights are still below freezing. Spring teases us in early March but never arrives before the predictable St. Patrick's Day snowstorm around March 17. Celebration-loving Quebecers have been known to parade through the streets of Montreal during a blinding blizzard rather than cancel the St. Patrick's Day parade, one of the biggest in the world.

In the cities on the quintessential early spring day, everyone takes to the streets for picnics on park benches, lunch in outdoor cafés and coffee on the steps of office towers, with coats flung open and scarves discarded.

The grass turns green about the end of April–**avril.** If you want to see a frantic Mother Nature, check out Quebec between late April and late May. The metamorphosis from white to brown to a million shades of green is nothing short of a miracle—and it happens every year! Apple blossoms pop open between the middle and the end of May–**mai.** Montreal and **la Montérégie** usually warm up a few days before the Eastern Townships. **La ville de Québec, les Laurentides,** and the other southern regions follow, and eventually a short but spectacular summer comes to the Far North.

THE ALL TOO SHORT SUMMER–L'ÉTÉ BIEN TROP COURT

Summer is officially here when school lets out, always before the Quebec national holiday, the feast of St. John the Baptist–**la St-Jean-Baptiste,** June 24. Quebecers get slightly schizoid at the start of summer with **la fête nationale** (of Quebec) on June 24 and Canada Day–**la fête du Canada** exactly one week later on July 1. Each holiday calls for a parade. The exuberance of celebrants is used as a barometer for politicians. In rural areas, the harvest of the first strawberries is celebrated, and it's been a few weeks since Quebecers shut off the heating system as an act of faith.

July–**juillet** is the month when most Quebecers take their holidays. The last two weeks of **juillet** are the "construction holidays". Many factories shut down, unionized construction crews pack it in, and workers and their families head for a lake or tend to chores left over from winter. Summer festivals abound, and for all practical purposes the government seems to close down.

Temperatures go as high as 35°C (95°F) in the summer in parts of southern Quebec. Away from the cities, it may be just as warm in the daytime but it is cooler in the evenings. Most businesses and stores have air conditioning–**la climatisation,** but only a few summer evenings are terribly uncomfortable. Most **Québécois** do not have **l'air climatisé** either in their cars or homes.

August–**août** (oo) brings a return to cool nights, fresh garden produce, especially corn–**blé-d'Inde** or **maïs sucré** and tomatoes–**tomates,** and back-to-school sales–**les soldes de la rentrée des classes** (for tourists combining a late summer trip with school shopping).

FALL AND ITS FOLIAGE–L'AUTOMNE ET SON FEUILLAGE

September–**septembre** brings the harvest and the splendid fall foliage arranged by Mother Nature–**Dame Nature.** The northern regions are aflame two to three weeks earlier than those along the American border. Colors here are every bit as spectacular as those in New England. After all, the Eastern Townships border Maine, New Hampshire and the Green Mountain State (**l'état des Montagnes vertes**–Vermont). (There's another memory hook: green is **vert**.)

October–**octobre** is shuffling through the dry leaves, views into woods unobstructed by leafy trees, a nip in the air, and cool afternoons by the fireside–**le foyer.**

WEATHER EXTREMES

There is no real "rainy" season in Quebec, but in summer we have some small local "twisters". It is unusual to have hurricanes or tornadoes. There are a few good summer storms with thunder–**le tonnerre** and lightning–**les éclairs** or **la foudre,** usually on very hot humid days in late June or early July. When conflicting weather systems collide we can have thunder and lightning in winter as well—now that is unusual!

Rarely do Quebecers lack a white Christmas–**Noël,** but it has happened—as have 15°C (60°F) days in February and 5°C (40°F) days in July. But we are accustomed to the seasons. We like to complain about the weather, and we invite you to come and do the same.

HOW TO DRESS FOR THE WEATHER?

On any day, it's important to be comfortably dressed for the activity you are contemplating. For example, if it's winter and you are going ice-fishing–**la pêche sur glace** or **la pêche blanche,** you won't be moving a lot and should wear several layers of clothing.

When it is very cold there won't be any slush except on the roads, and if you have lined footwear and many socks, you should be fine. Since **la voirie** puts salt and other chemicals on the roads to help melt the ice and form slush, the best all-purpose winter footwear–**chaussures** to keep you comfortable should be waterproof–**imperméables.** With the number of new synthetics on the market it is possible to keep your feet warm and dry.

For puddle-hopping in Montreal in the spring, go for lined rubber boots–**des bottes de caoutchouc.** If adventuring in **le Grand-Nord,** look for something warmer. For ski country, choose high boots. Those with a drawstring top are great for children.

Body heat is lost through the head–**la tête,** and a hat–**un chapeau** or **tuque** which pulls well down over the ears–**les oreilles** is essential on cold winter days. When skiing on the coldest ski days, there are face masks and "ski bums", fleece-lined squares for cold chair-lift seats. Mittens–**des mitaines** are usually warmer than gloves–**des gants.** Neck warmers, knitted tubes that slide down over the head and keep the neck warm, are called **faux-cols;** they are warm, can be pulled up over your nose and are easier to keep under control than scarves–**des foulards.** Dressing for the cold–**le froid** is best done by layering–**des couches.** You need fewer clothes for cross-country skiing–**le ski de fond** than for alpine skiing–**le ski alpin** because you are usually in more sheltered areas and you produce heat as you ski. You are also going slower, so there is less wind. If you put on several layers of clothing, you can always add or remove one as needed for comfort. Fur may no longer be politically correct for human beings, but there is no equal to fur for keeping warm.

By the time the month of May–**mai** rolls around, heavy clothes can be discarded. It is still good to keep layering and wear a windbreaker–**un blouson** or **un coupe-vent** (an anglicism) which can take a warm sweater–**un chandail** underneath it. Should it be very rainy–**très pluvieux,** you might want to have boots–**des bottes** and an umbrella–**un parapluie** on hand and possibly a raincoat–**un imperméable.** In June and July, Quebecers usually come out in shorts–**des shorts,** T-shirts–**des t-shirts,** and light summer wear–**des vêtements d'été.** August evenings–**des soirées du mois d'août** often warrant at least **un chandail,** and layering is back in style by mid-September–**mi-septembre.**

ADAPTING TO THE CLIMATE

We have suggested linguistic stages–**des étapes linguistiques** for your visit, and we would also suggest that you explore the province in climatic stages–**des étapes climatiques.** Spend a few weeks on the ski slopes or trails in January and February before venturing into **le Grand-Nord** for a winter vacation. You can try winter camping in many of Quebec's parks to test your gear and yourself in –40° weather. (Hospitals are easier to get to, if needed, in the south.) But come and learn more about this wonderful part of the world, both its climate and its language. **Bienvenue au Québec!**

SOME WEATHER-RELATED VOCABULARY

Weather forecast	**Prévisions météorologiques, la météo**
What's the forecast?	**C'est quoi, la météo?**
What's the weather like?	**Quel temps fait-il?**
The weather is great.	**Il fait beau. Le temps est beau.**
It's raining. It's snowing.	**Il pleut. Il neige.**
It's hot, cold, miserable!	**Il fait chaud, froid, mauvais!**
It's raining cats and dogs!	**Il pleut à boire debout!** (so you can drink standing up)
Is it warm enough?	**Est-ce qu'il fait assez chaud?**
In the hot weather	**Pendant les grandes chaleurs**
Weather permitting	**Si le temps le permet**
To weather a storm	**Survivre à une tempête**
Snowstorm	**Une tempête de neige**
Storm	**Un orage**
Thunderclap	**Un coup de tonnerre**
Lightning bolt	**La foudre**
Temperature	**La température**

There was a young man of Quebec
Who sat buried in snow to his neck.
When they asked, "Is you friz?"
He replied, "Yes, I is,
But we don't call this cold in Quebec."

CHAPTER 5

PEOPLE, POLITICS AND LANGUAGE

Quebec is sometimes referred to as the heart and soul of Canada, and most would agree it's often a palpitating heart and troubled soul. Still, the unique character of this French-speaking society is one of Canada's defining characteristics. And although more than three million Quebecers speak English, Quebec is a decidedly French society in both language and culture.

REAL QUEBECERS EAT POUTINE*

There are often heated debates about who are **les Québécois de souche** (old stock Quebecers) or **les Québécois pure laine** (pure wool Quebecers), that is, "real" Quebecers. But, as is true of most North Americans, only the people of the First Nations (the native peoples or aboriginals) can claim first ownership, and even they inherited lands from earlier tribes. As they say in **la Gaspésie,** we're all "friggin drifters".

FIRST WHITE SETTLERS

Since you have carefully read A DELIBERATELY ABRIDGED HISTORY OF QUEBEC, you'll recall that the first white residents of New France–**la Nouvelle-France** came

---

*__Poutine__ (pronounced pooh-teen) is a **québécois** fast food which ranks right up there with **'amburgers** and **'ot dogs** and is found at every roadside canteen–**casse-croûte.** It consists of layers of cheese curds, French fries and gravy.

from France. The French language–**le français** or **la langue française** was also imported from that country but has undergone substantial changes. In the '70s a government department was established to help rid the language of anglicisms and sloppy French referred to as **joual,** derived from careless pronunciation of the French word **cheval**–horse. If you learned your French at the Sorbonne, you might have a bit of difficulty understanding the lingo of the garage mechanic–**le garagiste,** but you will certainly be able to understand the broadcasters at Radio-Canada.

The population of the province is overwhelmingly white, especially in rural Quebec. However, as with most large cities all over the world, immigrants are changing the face of Quebec's large cities, particularly Montreal. It may be interesting to recall that the first black baseball player to play in the major leagues did so for the long gone triple-A team, the Montreal Royals. It was in Montreal that Jackie Robinson made his remarkable debut, largely because of the province's openness to other races and cultures.

STIRRING UP THE POT

After 1763 France paid little attention to the people and politics of Quebec until its president Charles de Gaulle stunned everyone by up-staging the World Exhibition in Montreal in 1967 with a grandiose performance from the balcony of City Hall. De Gaulle chose Canada's centenary to pronounce his support for an independent Quebec with his declaration **"Vive le Québec! Vive le Québec libre!"** (Long live Quebec! Long live free Quebec!) An outsider might have assumed Quebecers were living in some sort of bondage, but his diplomatic gaffe was generally attributed to plain bad manners, an audience, and a soap box.

YOU SPEAK ENGLISH WELL FOR A QUEBECER!

You may be surprised to be told that in Quebec, more people speak English–**l'anglais** than the total population of each of seven Canadian provinces. Where does this information come from? A 1990 study by the well known demographers Lachapelle and Dallaire noted that 54 per cent of English-speaking Quebecers speak French, and 30 per cent of French-speaking Quebecers speak English. Mathematically speaking, that means that about three million people here can communicate in English. Isn't that a relief!

Linguistically, Quebec residents are identified as anglophones, francophones or allophones. According to Webster's dictionary, anglophones are those "consisting of or belonging to an English-speaking population"; the French dictionary Larousse defines an anglophone as **"qui parle l'anglais"**–someone who speaks English. The same two sources declare that a francophone is "consisting of or belonging to a French-speaking population" or **"qui parle le français".** The meaning given to allophone in **la belle province** is "one whose mother tongue is neither English nor French", but this definition is not found in either dictionary. (There are also **les autochtones**–native people, but they're not a linguistic group.)

English-speaking Quebecers–**les anglophones** or **les anglos** make up about ten percent of Quebec's population. Large Italian, Greek, German and other ethnic communities representing many races and cultures share living space, particularly in and around Montreal. Quebec is further enriched by the presence of the native people: Cree, Inuit, and others. Numbers don't really tell the story. Because of the regional concentration of anglophones, the English-speaking minority is actually the majority in some small communities. For example, over 60 per cent of the population of **la ville de Lac Brome** (which includes Knowlton) use English as a first language; but the English-speaking population of the Townships is only about eight per cent.

For more than 200 years anglophones and francophones have lived side by side as good neighbors, often without ever learning to speak each other's language. However, today Quebec's young people—especially non-francophones—tend to be bilingual.

It may happen that newcomers to Quebec will be provoked by someone who does not want to provide services in English. If this should happen to you, flash a smile and say very slowly **"touriste"**–tourist, or **"en vacances"**–on vacation, and your luck might change. If not, vote with your feet and try someone who isn't having a bad day.

If you speak an accented English or French, it will automatically be assumed that you are able to speak the other of the two languages. A Polish friend never ceased to be amazed that when she asked a question in English, she would invariably be answered in French. If this should happen to you, just smile and try the word **touriste** again. On the other hand, a question in beginner's French will usually bring a reply in English.

WHAT IS AN OFFICIAL LANGUAGE?

In 1969, when Pierre Elliott Trudeau was Prime Minister of Canada, Canada enacted a law called the Official Languages Act. This law was drawn up after a study by the Pépin-Robarts Commission gobbled up many millions of Canadian taxpayers' dollars and concluded that persons speaking French or English should have the right to communicate with institutions of the federal government in their own language regardless of where they live in the country. The law decreed two official languages in Canada—French and English. It also laid down that federal civil servants should be able to serve the public in either official language wherever numbers warrant. The requisite number to warrant services was never firmly established, but it's safe to assume that visitors and residents should be able to find information in either French or English at any *federal* government park, post office, customs office, or airport.

Of the 10 provinces, eight use English–**l'anglais** as their established language. Only New Brunswick, immediately east of Quebec, with about one third of its people having French as their mother tongue, went a step further and declared itself a bilingual province, extending French and English language rights to provincial as well as federal public services.

In 1977 Quebec enacted Bill 101, ordaining French–**le français** as the official language of Quebec. However, federal institutions in Quebec continue to provide services in English, and it is possible to receive information and services in English from the Quebec government. The regional tourist guides and hunting and fishing rules, for example, are issued in English as well as French, and other documents are available in English upon request. In 1987, the Quebec government passed a law guaranteeing its citizens the right to receive health and social services in English from provincial health care institutions. This should provide some assurance to travellers as well as residents.

There is a conscious effort on the part of individuals to communicate with each other in either English or French depending on the circumstances. This may result in hilarious or embarrassing translations. When the French-language organizers of an agriculture fair wanted to advise English-speaking farmers that chickens must be inspected by a veterinarian before being shown, they posted the sign: "Farmers, if you plan to expose your bird at the fairgrounds, you must first have it inspected." A job opening for a seamstress was translated as **"un egout"**–a sewer for waste water. An advertising campaign to attract tourists to Montreal fell flat because itwas promoted as a city with an "attitude"—not a positive approach in English-speaking North America. A major gaffe resulted in a pool of journalists being referred to as **une piscine**–a swimming pool!

SO WHAT IS "NATIONAL"?

In Quebec, the term "national" is a label used to identify provincial properties and possibly to convey a larger political message. It's used for some tourist attractions and museums. The Canadian government has invested heavily in Quebec parks, historic sites and other institutions such as post offices. So when you are touring around **la belle province** and you see **national** (masculine) or **nationale** (feminine), check for the "national" symbol. A small maple leaf–**une feuille d'érable** (or possibly a stylized beaver–**un castor)** indicates it's federally sponsored; a large stylized lily–**une fleur de lis** shows it's a provincial endeavor. Where you see the maple leaf you should have no problem getting service in English. But don't be surprised to be greeted wherever you go by one of those three million **Québécois** who speak English.

QUEBEC LANGUAGE LEGISLATION

A generation ago, many English Quebecers had little reason to speak French. They attended English schools, worked in English offices and factories and were supported by church and social groups in a lively community.

Simply put, they saw no need to complicate their lives with a second language—even though it was the language of the majority of Quebecers.

The Quiet Revolution and **francisation** of Quebec with its language legislation, coupled with a declining English population and increasingly fragile institutional networks, prompted many anglophones to reassess their future in Quebec. English-speaking people left in a massive exodus following the election of the separatist **Parti Québécois** in 1976 and the adoption of the Charter of the French Language (Bill 101 or **la Charte de la langue française)** in 1977. But those "anglos" who opted to stay took a new approach to living in Quebec. They demanded intensive French-immersion programs in schools. As a result Quebec has long been a laboratory for second-language teaching experiments.

One of the objectives of the language laws was to oblige new immigrants to send their children to French schools. The debate is currently raging whether or not Quebec's schools should be structured along linguistic or "confessional" (sectarian) lines. The British North America Act (1867) made provision for Catholic and Protestant schools, and other religious denominations were, by and large, ignored. In the '50s and '60s, Protestants coming to Quebec from foreign countries were not admitted to Catholic schools; consequently, immigrant children attended Protestant (English) schools, and they became integrated into the English-speaking community.

With the advent of "the pill" and active feminism, Quebec's birth rate plummeted, and attention was paid to the precarious state of the French language in Quebec. The Charter of the French Language–**la Charte de la**

langue française obliges parents who have not been educated in English elementary schools in Canada to send their children to a French elementary or secondary school. (There are exceptions.) To reinforce the protection of the French language, the French majority accepted restrictions on their right to choose English as the language of education for their children.

SCHOOLING–L'ENSEIGNEMENT

English schools begin teaching French in kindergarten, while in the French system, English is introduced in Grade 4. Quebec children who are five by September 30 may enroll in kindergarten. There are six grades in elementary school and five in secondary school, so the student finishes secondary school after Grade 11. French secondary schools refer to the high school years as **Secondaire I, II, III, IV et V.**

As mentioned above, francophones, anglophones from outside of Canada and allophones are all required by Quebec law to send their children to French elementary and secondary schools. English-speaking Quebecers may send their children to either French or English elementary or secondary schools, an option which has made young anglophones today's most bilingual Quebecers. Many senior anglophones remain unilingual, while many older francophones are bilingual, some having spent their working lives employed by unilingual anglophones. And allophones, seizing the opportunity provided in a bilingual country, tend to be multilingual.

At present, any student who has the academic requirements can attend college or university in either language without restriction. Junior colleges are called **CEGEPs** (pronounce it say-zhep), which is short for **Collège d'Enseignement Général et Professionel.**

French Second Language courses, usually called FSL, are available from public and private institutions as well as places like the YMCA. Special FSL courses are available to immigrants. English Second Language courses, ESL programs, are very popular among the francophones. Most of us agree that knowing more than one language is an asset.

A WORD ABOUT APOSTROPHES

As innocuous as an apostrophe may appear to an outsider, in the perception of many non-French-speaking Quebecers the high curl symbolized an unjust restriction of their rights when the Quebec government passed Bill 101, a law banning outdoor commercial signs in languages other than French. Because the apostrophe is not used in French to denote possession, words such as "Eaton's" and "Joe's" were considered English and illegal. Eaton's in Quebec is now simply Eaton. Satirists have speculated that a creative entrepreneur might find a new use for warehouses full of apostrophes.

AND ABOUT SWEARING

The Catholic Church gets credit for being the inspiration for many of the epithets used by French-speaking Quebecers. We also call on the Lord's help, or chastise him: "My lord!" is **Mon Dieu!** There is no English equivalent for swear words derived from consecrated altar adornments and articles used in the celebration of the Catholic mass, such as **tabarnac, criss, câlice, 'ostie.**

"Fuck" in its many tenses and senses is used as freely and frequently in French conversation as it is in English, but it doesn't have the same feeling as in English. **Maudit**–damn and **merde**–shit are also frequently heard, but a real **Québécois** says **marde** as in **mange la marde!** for the latter.

There is a word that can be used to describe all kinds of things, and its English equivalent means disgusting or revolting. Young people use this constantly and shorten it from **dégueulasse** (day-gull-ass) to **dégueu.** No doubt you will hear it often. And some people use **cacahuète** (peanut) for an oath!

TRY IT, YOU'LL LIKE IT!

Most visitors to Quebec are well served in either language, especially in the urban areas in southwest Quebec. To fully appreciate a visit to Quebec, we recommend that you give the French language a try and **parler** with the locals in their own language. You'll probably find it easier than you think to rendezvous with **les Québécois** in **les bistros, restaurants** and **sites historiques.** Enjoy yourself! **Amusez-vous bien!**

Start with a few simple phrases:

Bonjour. Ça va bien?	Hi. Everything (going) OK?
Comment ça va?	How are things?
Ça va?	Everything okay?
Bonne journée.	Have a nice day.
C'est le fun!	Fun, eh?
La toilette?	Where is the bathroom?
Oui. Non.	Yes. No.
S'il vous plaît	Please
Merci	Thank you
Merci beaucoup.	Thank you very much.

POLITICS–LA POLITIQUE

Politics is a serious sport for Quebecers, and a short introduction to the sport will help you orient yourself. About 20 years ago, several political parties were vying for the favors of **les Québécois.** Since much of Quebec politics revolves around the question of francophone nationalism and the possible separation of Quebec from Canada, the political parties spend much time debating this one issue, and the provincial parties, instead of being liberals or conservatives, or right wing or left wing, are labelled federalist or separatist.

Both the federal and Quebec governments are elected for a maximum five-year term. Sometimes the leader of the ruling party will deem the moment opportune, dissolve the government before the five-year term is up and call a quick election. More often in the fourth year of a government's mandate it will start looking for the perfect moment to call an election and will either start giving out lots of goodies to the ridings (electoral districts) or make favorable contract settlements with government workers just before calling one. "They're surfacing the roads—must be an election coming."

Since September 1993, Canada has had a Liberal government led by Jean Chrétien, and Quebecers have been represented in Ottawa by 75 elected Members of Parliament (MPs): 20 from the Liberal Party of Canada, one Progressive Conservative, one Independent, and 53 **Bloc Québécois,** a Quebec separatist party. The Quebec National Assembly is composed of 125 members, **Membres de l'Assemblée Nationale (députés):** 47 from the federalist Quebec Liberal Party, led by Daniel Johnson, 77 from the separatist **Parti Québécois,** now led by Premier Lucien Bouchard, and one held by a young man in the middle, Mario Dumont of the **Parti**

d'Action Démocratique du Québec (ADQ). These **députés** were elected in September 1994 and should be in office until 1999.

Municipal politics peak in early November, when municipal elections take place. The mayor–**le maire** and the councillors–**les conseillers** are elected the first Sunday in November, usually for a four-year term. In small municipalities the council is composed of only seven members, a mayor and six councillors.

A POST-MODERN SOCIETY

Quebec society is touted as being **avant-gardiste,** with some of the most progressive legislation on social issues in North America.

In Quebec for several years now, with the approval of the women's movement, the law has required women to retain their maiden names–**leur nom de fille** after marriage–**après le mariage.** Apart from causing confusion for older married women who if hospitalized are registered under their maiden names, and for everyone trying to remember two surnames for one married couple, it seems to work well. It keeps things clear in this day of multiple marriages but gives rise to multiple hyphenated surnames. Children born in Quebec can officially use a combination of the mother's name and the father's name (or either name). Two individuals each bearing hyphenated surnames will have fun when they marry and come to name their own children.

RELATIONS AND OTHER FOLKS

With all the changes in social legislation in Quebec it is useful to know some of the common terminology related to people–**les gens.** Families–**les familles** can be headed by a man–**un homme** and/or a woman–**une femme.** These two people are partners–**des conjoints; un**

conjoint is male, **une conjointe** is female. They may be married–**mariés** or single–**célibataires** (but not necessarily celibate). A husband–**un mari** or **un époux** and a wife–**une épouse** have in-laws–**des beaux-parents.** A mother is **une mère** and a mother-in-law is **une belle-mère;** a grandmother is **une grand-mère.** A daughter-in-law is **une bru,** a son-in-law is **un gendre.** ***Les Belles-Soeurs*** is a famous play by Michel Tremblay about sisters-in-law.

A father–**un père** may also be a father-in-law–**un beau-père** and/or a grandfather–**un grand-père.** A baby–**un bébé** grows up to be a child–**un enfant**. A son is **un fils** (pronounced fiss), a daughter–**une fille** (pronounced fee-y); so a grandson is **un petit-fils,** a granddaughter–**une petite-fille,** and grandchildren are **des petits-enfants.**

A boy is **un garçon,** a girl is **une fille,** and if they are brother and sister they are **frère** and **soeur.** Aunts and uncles are **des tantes** et **des oncles,** cousins are **des cousins et cousines,** and the relatives are **des parents.** (**Un parent** is not necessarily a parent.) Close friends and relations are **des proches.** Teenagers are **des adolescents** or **des ados** for short. **Les ados** usually refer to boyfriends as **les chums** and girlfriends as **les blondes.** Friends are **des amis** and **des amies** or **des copains et copines.** Roommates are **co-locateurs** (co-renters) or **co-locs** for short. Older friends are referred to as **des compagnons** or **des compagnes.**

Singers are **les chanteurs** or **chanteuses,** TV stars are **les comédiens** or **les comédiennes,** stars are **les vedettes.** Famous people are **les célébrités,** politicians are **les politiciens;** and **les Québécois** call themselves **"un peuple"**–a people.

CHAPTER 6

LET'S GO! LET'S SPEAK FRENCH!

Be grateful you are tackling a language that has the same characters as those of the English language. You are not launching into Arabic, Japanese or Russian. French uses the same 26 letters as English, but with the combination of letters and accents there are about 36 different sounds in French. Pity the poor bloke learning English. Try to explain the logic behind the sounds of these English words: bough, cough, rough, though, through, thorough, fought. How about pouch and touch, or river and driver?

THE NON-DEFINITIVE PRONUNCIATION KEY

It's sometimes easier to understand the written than the spoken word because many word roots are the same in both languages. So it's important to learn a few basic rules of pronunciation in order to understand and be understood. When the bus driver calls out the name of a street, knowing how it sounds as well as how it looks gets you off at the right stop.

Take **Pie IX** for instance. A couple of main streets in Montreal are named after popes. More than one Catholic pope was called Pius, which in French is **Pie,** pronounced "pea" as in pea soup, not "pie" as in apple pie. So if you're looking for **Pie IX** don't expect the bus driver to say Pie Nine; he'll call out **Pie neuf** (pea nuf). (The

Botanical Garden in Montreal is at **Pie IX** and Sherbrooke St. East.) A major boulevard in Montreal is named after René Lévesque, the late well-known Quebec leader. To an English ear, René Lévesque sounds like Rainy Leveck.

Like English, French has silent letters. Some letter combinations sound entirely different in the two languages. You will find it easier to understand the sounds if you listen to the language a bit. Watching the news on the French television channel is an interesting exercise, if you read lips and listen to the French voice-over. Actually the French stations use a combination of sub-titles, summary translations and the actual English voice on newscasts, an interesting mix.

Let's go! **Allons-y!**

VOWEL SOUNDS*

Spelling in French	English sound	French word	English pronunciation
au, -eau	-oh	**beau**	boh
-é, -er, -ez	-a as in "Abe"	**bébé**	baybay

These two combinations come up very often and if you can only remember two vowel sounds, try to remember these. The letter **-é** appears as the last letter in many words, particularly in verbs.

A classic example is **ferme** and **fermé. Une ferme** using English phonetics sounds like "fair-meh" with the **eh** as just a whisper, and means "a farm". **Fermé** comes from the verb **fermer** (to close). It's pronounced "fair-may" with the same stress on each syllable. You may see

*In speaking English we tend to stretch vowels, so that "grapes" may sound like "gray apes". French speakers make the vowels sharp and short—so don't lengthen them.

fermé on stores once they've closed for the day. In Quebec we anglophones often "close the lights"–**nous fermons les lumières,** meaning we turn off the lights, and **nous ouvrons les lumières**–"we open them", much to the chagrin of some English speakers.

Spelling in French	English sound	French word	English pronunciation
-a	-a sound in "sat"	**banane**	ba-nan
-â	-ah	**gâteau**	gah-toh
-è, -ê	-e sound in "ebb"	**scène**	sen
-eu, -oeu	-eu sound like "er" without the "r"	**eux**	eu
-**i**	-ee sound in "peel"	**Paris**	pa-ree
-ô	-o sound in "ode"	**tôt**	toe
-o	-u sound in "but"	**poste**	pust (rhymes with bust)
-ou	-oo sound in "ooze"	**route**	root
-u	-u sound halfway between "prune" and "few"	**brume**	brewm

Words are traded, borrowed, and downright plundered from one language to another. Did you know that O.K. (okay) is said to come from the French **au quai?** It means "to the wharf", and in the days when most freight was transported by ship, once a crate was ready someone might yell **"Au quai!"** Sailors adopted another

French word when they met trouble at sea. The international cry for "Help" is "Mayday", possibly from the French "help me"–**m'aider.**

NASAL VOWEL SOUNDS

These following four sounds are nasal sounds. Hold your nose and don't let the tip of your tongue touch the teeth, and they'll sound right.

Spelling in French	English sound	French word	English pronunciation
-am, -an, -em, -en	ahn holding nose (anh)	**sans**	sanh
im, -in, -yn, -ym, -aim, -ain, -eim, -ein	-en holding nose (enh)	**bain**	benh (ben without the **n**)
-om, -on	-own holding nose (onh)	**fond**	phone (without the **-ne**—fonh)
-um, -un	unh as in unh huh	**parfum**	par-funh

CONSONANTS

There are other pronunciation caprices of the French language. Like the cockney English speakers, francophones don't pronounce the letter **h,** and **th** is pronounced **t.** This explains why the "Heathers" of Quebec become accustomed to being called "Eater". A young man from France sent the English family he lived with into gales of laughter when he'd announce "I'm hungry." In French the **h** is silent, and his announcement always came out "I'm angry". There's a situation where body language says more than words.

c before **e**, **i** or **y** is like **s** in sing: **difficile**–dee-fee-seel (difficult). In all other cases, **c** sounds like **k**: **crêpe** (pancake)–krep.

ç makes a hissing **s** sound: **français**–franh-seh (French).

ch sounds like **sh: chambre** (room) is pronounced shanh-br'. "Chat" is a perfectly good English word meaning a light conversation, but **chat** (sha) is a very different French word meaning cat. Note that the **t** in **chat** is silent. This commonly happens to consonants at the ends of words. In short words they are often sounded: **avec** (with), **cher** (dear), **oeuf** (egg), **quel** (which). **(C, r, f,** and **l** usually are sounded at the ends of words—so be **CaReFuL**!)

g before **e, i** or **y** is like **s** in measure: **rouge**–roozh (red). But **g** before any other letter is like **g** in goat: **garage**–ga-razh (same word in both languages—garage).

gn is like **ny** in canyon: **espagnol**–ess-pa-nyol (Spanish).

h is silent: **hôtel** is pronounced oh-tel (hotel–a form of **hébergement**–lodging).

j is pronounced like the **z** in azure, as in **je**–zhuh (I). **Je sais**–zhuh say (I know).

ll is usually pronounced like **y** in yes: **famille**–fa-meey (family). Exceptions: **ville** (veel), **village** (vee-lazh).

qu and **q** are usually pronounced as **k: qui** (who) is sounded as kee.

r is rolled like a dry gargle.

s between two vowels sounds like the **z** of zero: **rose** (pink) is pronounced rohz (like "rose" in English).

Unless the word following begins with a vowel, most final or terminal consonants are silent, especially **d, t,**

s, x, and **z.** Example: **dent** (tooth) pronounced danh But . . . if you have a vowel starting the next word, the silent consonant comes back to life and becomes part of the following word: so **ils ont** (they have) is pronounced eel-zonh, and **sans argent** (without money) becomes sanh-zar-zhanh, not to be confused with **sans frais**– without charge, free.

The easiest way to feel comfortable with the language is to read things like road and commercial signs. As you're driving along Quebec highways, use the opportunity to read billboards and road signs aloud. Quebec language laws require that French must be the dominant language on all outdoor commercial signs, but other languages are sometimes permitted.

PUTTING FRENCH WORDS TOGETHER

First and foremost, all French nouns have gender. This is shown by the word for "the": **le** (masculine) or **la** (feminine). If you can't think of the French word for something just say **le** or **la** and throw in an English word, and your listeners will understand what you are trying to say. This works particularly well if your car breaks down. The garage attendant will understand perfectly if you say you need **"le towing"** or that you have **"une flat". "Garagiste"** is a language unto itself spoken in most parts of Quebec.

Quebec has a government authority called the **Office de la langue française (OLF)** which is devoted to protecting and purifying the French language by encouraging proper use of French and ridding it of commonly used anglicisms. **"Le towing",** then, is correctly **le remorquage,** and **"une flat"**–a flat tire is **une crevaison** or **un pneu crevé.** But just as the restaurateur knows that **un hambourgeois** is a hamburger, Quebec mechanics know just what you mean by "le crankshaft" and "le fan belt". They had to learn car repair using American manuals and know the terms.

French people are Latin in temperament and use their arms to gesture a lot—so, if all else fails, throw your arms in the air and say **"C'est tout fucké!"** (This is not as rude in French as in English.) Shrugging your shoulders is also a well understood form of body language.

If you are a beginner at French, don't lose time trying to determine if a noun is masculine or feminine. Alternate **le** and **la** and listen carefully to the person you are speaking with to hear which they use. If you know a third language and figure that because table is masculine in Hebrew it should be **"le table"** in French, you'll be wrong because table in French is **"la table".** Why a house is feminine **(la maison)** and a boat (which we usually refer to in English as "she") is masculine in French **(le bateau)** is a mystery. So don't worry about second-guessing every noun.

Since French nouns are either masculine or feminine, adjectives modifying them have the same gender as the nouns. Some of us have a handful of asexual adjectives in our repertoire, such as **magnifique, formidable, terrible.** Did you notice that they are almost identical to the English words and mean the same thing? Put on a Maurice Chevalier accent, and **voilà,** you're speaking French—man-yee-feek, for-me-dabl, ter-reebl!

Another thing about adjectives: in French they mostly follow the noun. **Un chandail vert**–a green sweater, **des mains froides**–cold hands. But some short ones precede the noun: **un beau jour, le bon garçon.**

Le, la, les are the equivalent of "the"; **un** or **une** and **des** are the equivalent of "a" or "an" and "some".

Just as many of us have personal signs at our houses such as "The Smiths", so Quebecers hang signs with things like **Les Tremblay.** (In French the family name is never made plural; the Jacksons are **les Jackson.)** A visitor once observed that an extraordinary number of **Québécois** were called Les!

SOME ESSENTIAL EXPRESSIONS

The publisher of an Edmonton newspaper once said that in 12 years of French lessons at school, the only phrase he mastered was : **"J'ai perdu ma plume dans le jardin de ma tante."** (I lost my pen in my aunt's garden.) The phrase isn't even a decent ice-breaker unless you need to borrow a pen.

Some useful expressions to know:

Excusez-moi or **je m'excuse**	Excuse me
S'il vous plaît (seel-voo-play)	Please
Merci, merci beaucoup (mair-see boh-koo)	Thank you, thank you very much
Où est la toilette? (oo eh la twa-lett)	Where is the washroom?

Most Quebec anglophones who learned French in English school were told that bathroom was **la salle de bain.** If you want to take a bath, by all means ask for **la salle de bain;** otherwise ask for **la toilette** or **les toilettes.**

Bonjour! Allo! (slang)	Hello, good day!
Bonne journée!	Have a good day!
Bonsoir! Bonne soirée!	Good evening! Have a nice evening!
Bonne nuit!	Good night!
Au revoir! Salut! (slang)	Goodbye! So long!
À la prochaine!	Till we meet again, till the next time

À bientôt!	See you soon!
Tournez à gauche	Turn left
À droite	To the right
Continuez tout droit, tout droit	Continue straight, straight ahead
À cinq minutes	Five minutes away
À pied	On foot
Là, là-bas	There, over there
Arrivée	Arrival
Départ	Departure
Fin	The end (e.g., of the road)
Fermé	Closed
Ouvert	Open

QUESTIONS, QUESTIONS (kest-y-onh)

A good newspaper reporter needs those famous six questions: Who? What? When? Where? Why? How? They may also come in handy if you are lost.

Qui? (kee)	Who?
Quoi? (kwa)	What?
Quand? (kanh)	When?
Où? (oo)	Where?
Pourquoi? (poor-kwa)	Why?
Comment? (kum-menh)	How?
Combien? (kunh-byenh)	How much?
À quelle distance?	How far?
Pardon? (par-donh)	I beg your pardon?
Parlez-vous l'anglais? (par-lay voo lanh-gleh)	Do you speak English?

ANSWERS–RÉPONSES (ray-pawnhss)

Moi–lui–elle–eux (mwa–lwee–ell–eu)	Me–him–her–them
Désolé	Sorry

Je ne sais pas (zhuh nuh say pa)	I don't know
Je ne comprends pas (zhuh nuh konh-pranh pa)	I don't understand
Hier; aujourd'hui (ee-air; oh-zhoor-dwee)	Yesterday; today
Demain (duh-menh)	Tomorrow
Le mois prochain	Next month
Le mois passé	Last month
La semaine prochaine	Next week
La semaine passée	Last week
L'an prochain, l'an passé	Next year, last year
Bientôt (byenh-toh)	Soon
Dans quelques minutes	In a few minutes
De rien (duh ree-enh)	It's nothing
Un peu (unh peu)	A little
Assez (ass-say)	Enough
Trop (troh)	Too much
Un instant! or **Minute!** (unh enh-stanh, mee-newt)	Wait a minute!
Encore (enh-kor)	Again
Lentement (lenh-t'-menh)	Slowly

VERBS

The two most important verbs in French are to be–**être,** and to have–**avoir.** It's a bit of a nuisance, but the verbs change with the subject. (Well, some perverse verbs do that in English: I am, you are, he is.)

The present tense of **être**–"to be" is:

I am–**je suis** (zhuh swee)	we are–**nous sommes** (noo-sum)
you are–**tu es** (one person) (tew eh)	you are–**vous êtes** (voo-zet)
she/he/it is–**elle/il est** (ell/eel eh)	they are–**ils/elles sont** (eel/ell ssonh)

I am tired.	**Je suis fatigué.**
He is lost.	**Il est perdu.**

and **avoir**–"to have":

I have–**j'ai** (zhay)	we have–**nous avons** (noo-za-vonh)
you have–**tu as** (one person) (tew a)	you have–**vous avez** (voo-za-vay)
she/he/it has–**elle/il a** (ell/eel a)	they have–**ils/elles ont** (eel/ell-zonh)

You have a dog.	**Vous avez un chien.**
They have the tickets.	**Ils ont les billets.**
I have no money.	**Je n'ai pas d'argent.**

NOTE: the negative is usually shown by **ne** before the verb and **pas** after it. The negative message will usually be understood if you use just the **ne.**

Just when you get the hang of it, along come the exceptions:

We're hungry.	**Nous avons faim.**	(We have hunger.)
I am twenty.	**J'ai vingt ans.**	(I have 20 years.)

Other important verbs include **aimer:** to like or love. Remember the song "Darling, **je vous aime beaucoup."** A nice thought, but in French, the formal **vous** is reserved for elders, the bishop, or school teachers. You'd use the more familiar **tu** or **te** to say, "Darling, **je t'aime beaucoup"**–I love you very much.

Still, it's a good idea to use **vous** all the time or until you get more familiar with the language. So **Avez-vous l'heure?** means "Do you have the time?" **Voulez-vous visiter le musée?** Would you like to visit the museum? **Voulez-vous** means "Do you want" or "Would you like". **Voulez-vous danser avec moi?** Would you like to dance with me? **Vous voulez** means "You want" or

"You would like".* "I want" or "I would like" is **Je veux.** I want a cup of coffee–**je veux un café.** Look out for **demander**–to ask; **une demande** is only a request, not an ultimatum!

The last useful verb we'll bring up is "to need", in French "to have need of": I have need of–**j'ai besoin de.** I need a dentist–**j'ai besoin d'un dentiste.**

ABOUT PROPER NAMES

In English we often add "a" to a man's name to make a woman's name such as Edwin–Edwina, Philip–Philippa, etc. In French we add an extra "e" and sometimes double the consonant, as in **Daniel–Danielle, André–Andrée, François–Françoise. Jean** (John) is a common man's name in French, and so is **Jean-Marie.** So if you are a woman named Jean call yourself **Jeanne** (zhan). There are unisex names such as **Dominique.** And there's the way French place-names often reverse the English order: James Bay–**Baie James,** Johnny's Garage–**Garage Johnny;** St. Luke's hospital–**Hôpital St-Luc.** All these little oddities will keep you on your toes.

Let's go! **Allons-y!** (al-lonh-zee)

*Notice that to ask a question you just reverse the order of the subject and verb: **vous allez**–you are going; **allez-vous?**–Are you going?

CHAPTER 7

ON THE ROAD AND ON THE SIDELINES

New Englanders eager to hit the ski slopes may think they've reached highway nirvana when they see road signs indicating the speed limit. Afraid not. As in the rest of Canada, all road signs indicate distances in the International System–**Système International (SI),** that is, kilometers or meters. As a rule of thumb, 60 miles per hour is about 100 kilometers per hour, and most speed limits are 100 kilometers per hour on main highways, 80 (50 mph) on secondary roads, and 50 (30 mph) through towns and villages.

Quebec provincial police–**la Sûreté du Québec (la SQ)** patrol highways and main arteries, while municipal police officers hand out tickets in towns and villages within their own territory. Both have a penchant for lurking in church yards. Quebec also benefits from the services of the Royal Canadian Mounted Police, the fabled RCMP–**la Gendarmerie Royale du Canada, la GRC,** which oversees drug-related crimes, illegal immigration, and other matters of federal jurisdiction.

RULES OF THE ROAD

Unlike some other parts of the world, you may *not* turn right on a red light in Quebec, and radar detectors are prohibited. You should know, too, that the devil-may-care attitude of Quebecers as pedestrians–**comme**

piétons has led them to totally ignore traffic signal lights. However, seat belts and motorcycle helmets are *obligatory* here, and well over 90 per cent of Quebecers respect these safety measures.

As the result of another safety measure, all newer cars and all motorcycles are equipped with running lights, i.e., the headlights are on when the car is operating. At busy intersections you will often see a flashing green light to indicate you can turn left. The sign for this will say **Priorité de virage au clignotement du feu vert**–you have priority when turning if the green light is flashing.

If stopped by a police officer from **la SQ, la Sûreté du Québec,** you will be asked to show your driver's license–**votre permis de conduire** and the car's registration–**l'enregistrement** or simply your papers–**vos papiers.** If you've been involved in a car accident, you will also be asked to show your insurance certificate–**la preuve d'assurance,** possibly to an irate Quebecer flailing his arms and yelling something that sounds like **mo-dee-tabernak-tay-foo-tway?** the joual version of Excuse me, but are you crazy?

ROAD SIGNS

Les Québécois have an artistic bent, and the folks who work for the roads department–**le ministère des Transports** have been particularly creative in devising a series of pictograms. Most of them are internationally recognized symbols, but the odd one may be as comprehensible as abstract art.

Some globally accepted terms and symbols used in public signage include **P** for Parking Area–**Aire de stationnement, H** for Hospital–**Hôpital,** and **?** indicating tourist information–**Information touristique.**

STOP ALREADY

Quebec's most celebrated sign is the stop sign—a red octagon emblazoned with the word **ARRÊT** or **STOP,** but not both. The stop sign at street corners in Quebec became the first tangible indication that the government intended to enforce its language laws in even the tiniest town and village. Signmakers were busy changing all **STOPs** to **ARRÊTs** for a number of years. The innocuous little sign was alternately a symbol of pride or oppression and created a surge in the spray-paint business. **ARRÊT** became **A R T** and **STOP** became **101.** We practice creative graffiti here.

Some purists argued that even in France **STOP** is the acceptable term for "put on the brakes", and **stop** appears in most French dictionaries as the command form of the verb **stopper.** Still, it was considered a nasty anglicism by the **Office de la langue française.**

What the Larousse dictionary considers a perfectly legitimate French verb was banned from the octagonal red sign and replaced by **ARRÊT,** a noun. More recently, it was decided that indeed **STOP** is a legitimate French word, and lo and behold, it is once again permitted on red octagonal signs in Quebec. Whew!

PARKING TIPS AND OTHER USEFUL SUGGESTIONS

If you are in a city and are curious about the parking limitations, assume that if signs are posted, *all* the restrictions apply. Suppose you stop beside a telephone pole, home to a number of signs. One shows a red circle with a large **P** and a line across it with **10h–1130h,** another says **lun–mer–ven,** and yet another says **Excepté le corps diplomatique.** There are three restrictions, and unless you are a member of the diplomatic corps don't even dream of parking here. Even if you have a diplomatic license you cannot park between 10:00 and 11:30 in the morning on Mondays, Wednesdays or Fridays. **Lun** is short for **lundi** (Monday), **mer** for **mercredi** (Wednesday), and **ven** for **vendredi** (Friday). The other days of the week are Tuesday–**mardi** abbreviated **mar,** Thursday–**jeudi (jeu),** Saturday–**samedi (sam),** and Sunday–**dimanche (dim).**

In the winter, you may find a sandwich board or a small signpost perched on a snowbank with the red circle around a **P** with a diagonal line through it. This indicates that a snow clearing crew is coming along, and your car had better not be in the way or it will be towed to a pound—and its ransom will be costly.

FURRY ROAD HAZARDS

In rural areas of the province, abundant wildlife constitutes a road hazard. The pictures of deer–**les chevreuils** in flight are not there to attract hunters. They denote deer crossings. Quebec's Eastern Townships region has the second largest deer population in Canada, and a doe, probably followed by her fawns, can be found crossing well travelled roads as well as remote ones. Deer tend to make paths for themselves, and civilization may interfere with these paths. It's hard to say when you are most likely to encounter wildlife on the roads, but the animals tend to be active at dusk and on clear bright nights. Some people swear that deer wait by the crossing signs before flinging themselves in front of cars which have absolutely no chance of stopping in time.

A moose–**un orignal** or a bear–**un ours** will do a lot more damage to the ordinary car than a deer, but an encounter with any of these creatures is to be avoided. Should one block your way, it's best to wait until it wanders off. Porcupines–**les porcs-épics,** raccoons–**les ratons laveurs,** and skunks–**les moufettes** or **les bêtes puantes** meet their demise in large numbers on country roads. The small animals are particularly abundant in early spring when they forage for food. The aroma of a dead skunk lingers for a long time.

PLACE NAMES

There are some quaint names of towns in Quebec, and the excellent tourist guides may give you their origins. Your trusty road map of the province will indicate that there are probably more saints per square mile here than anywhere else in the world. After exhaustive research it has been determined that according to the Quebec road map–**la carte routière du Québec** there are over 500 towns named after saints.

On the map–**la carte** there are 47 towns that start with the letter **S,** and over 550 under the section **St** or **Ste** **(Ste** being the feminine form of **St).** Let's look at a couple of examples. (We could start with **St-Adolphe-**

de Howard or **Ste-Agnès-de-Dundee.)** Under **St-F** there are **St-François (Île d'Orléans), St-François-(Montmagny), St-François d'Assise, St-François-de-Masham, St-François-de-Sales, St-François-du-lac.** Now for the girls: **Ste-Françoise (Lotbinière), Ste-Françoise (Rivière-du-Loup);** back to the gentlemen: **St-François-Xavier-de-Brompton, St-François-Xavier-de-Viger.** Confused? There are also ten variations on **Ste-Anne** including two **Ste-Anne-du-lac** and one **Ste-Anne-des-lacs.** Be vigilant. Just think how much fun you can have getting lost in a region where not too many folks speak English. It's sure to be something you could write in your memoirs.

Not all our ancestors were saints. There's a town called **St-Louis-du-Ha-Ha** (reportedly christened by some poor explorer named Louis who laughed when he discovered he was not on a river but in a bay with no outlet.) Then there's **St-Pierre-de-Vérone-à-Pike-River,** a tiny town near Lake Champlain which until recently was called Pike River after the river which runs through it. The parish is **St-Pierre-de-Vérone,** and so unsuspecting people looking for Pike River (the town) now must find **St-Pierre-de-Vérone-à-Pike-River,** which is so long a name you're through the town before you've finished reading it. Pike River (the river) is now called **la rivière aux Brochets.**

In Montreal a downtown cross-street was named after one of the city's first bishops: Bishop Mountain. Unfortunately the city fathers turned the street name Mountain into the word mountain–**de la Montagne.** Today a toponomy commission oversees the naming of streets, mountains, and important landmarks, and they try to use names that are significant to the local populations. The English community is vigilant in safeguarding place names honoring its pioneers. Surely Bishop Mountain has been remembered elsewhere in the province.

ROADWAY SIGNS

Arrêt d'autobus–Bus stop
Attendez le signal–Wait for the signal
Autoroute–Expressway
Barrée–the access or the road is blocked
Belvédère–a lookout, also indicated by a pictogram of a person with a telescope
Cédez–Yield
Centre commercial or **centre d'achats**–shopping mall or shopping center
Centre-ville–Downtown
Chemin–Road
Chemin de fer–Railway
Circulation locale seulement–Local traffic only
CLSC–**Centre Local des Services Communautaires**–a local health clinic or doctor's office
Cul-de-sac–Dead end or No exit
Danger–Danger
Défense de passer–You can't go that way, No passing
Dégel (a sign of spring)–Thaw. Good idea to stay off dirt roads if you see this one. A pictogram of a truck tightening a belt around it tells truckers to lighten their loads in the period of thaw.
Détour–take off the accent and it's a detour
Dynamitage—Fermez votre émetteur–Dynamite zone—shut off your transmitters, radio
Economusée–a rural industry museum where you can buy the products produced
Entrée interdite–Do not enter
Érablière–Sugar shack where you may purchase maple products
Étang–Pond

Excepté véhicules autorisés–Authorized vehicles only
Fermé–Closed. (Take off the accent and you have **Ferme**–Farm.)
Fermez vos phares–Turn off your headlights. At the end of a tunnel there is often a large sign **Vos phares?**–Did you turn your lights off?
Fin–The end, usually of a numbered highway
Fin de sens unique–End of one-way section
Fin des voies rapides–End of the fast lanes, the expressway
Gabarit–clearance
Île–Island
Interdit–Prohibited/Forbidden/No/Not here
Lac–Lake; **Bord du lac**–Lakeshore
Lentement–Slowly
Ligne d'arrêt–The stop line at an intersection
Métro–The subway in Montreal (but **Metro** is a supermarket chain)
Mont or **Montagne**–A mountain
Moulin–Mill
Musée–Museum
Ouvert–Open
Ouvert quand les feux clignotent–A sign along with a picture of a truck hanging itself indicates a weigh station where trucks are required to stop when the lights are flashing.
Parc–Park
Piste de ski–Ski trail
Piste cyclable–Bicycle path
Plage–Beach
Pont–Bridge (very important on the island of Montreal)
Pont couvert–Covered bridge (there are still a few left), usually indicated by a pictogram
Port–The same in both languages, where the big

ships come in

Préparez-vous à arrêter–Be prepared to stop

Priorité de virage au clignotement du feu vert–A gem that means you have priority to turn left when the green light is flashing.

Ralentissez–Slow down

Rang–A country road or range

Reculez–Back up—you are going the wrong way!

Risque de brouillard–Risk of FOG. On some stretches of highway in low-lying areas, particularly in the dramatic temperature changes in fall or spring, fog can be a very real danger.

Route–Highway

Rue–Street

Saisonnier, -ière–Seasonal

Sentier pédestre–Hiking trail

Site historique, lieu historique–Historic site

Sortie–Exit. **3 prochaines sorties**–Next three exits

Sûreté du Québec–Police is an indication of a police station manned by the provincial police. Most large cities have their own police forces as well.

Surveillance aérienne–Airplanes might be watching you.

Traversier–Ferry (a seasonal service)

Urgence santé is emblazoned on ambulances and emergency vehicles in Montreal.
Urgence–emergency, **santé**–health

Virage–turn

Vitesse–speed. **La vitesse tue**–Speed kills

Voie–Lane. **Voie réservée**–Reserved lane
Une voie seulement–one lane only

?–Tourist information

ON THE SIDELINES

Do your best to stay healthy while here. But if you have the misfortune to have an accident or become ill, be assured that most major hospital centers provide medical services in English. In fact, even in smaller communities, there are few, if any, hospitals where services are not available in English.

In 1987, Quebec passed legislation guaranteeing access to health and social services to English-speaking Quebecers in their own language where there is a significant demand. While there are some gaps in the system, they are unlikely to be large enough to fall through. In any case, Ow, Ouch, Oy! Oy! and successive swear words are universally recognized as indicators of pain.

MEDICAL SERVICES

If you are from another Canadian province, your Medicare card will be honored. If you are from the U.S., welcome to socialized medicine! Residents of countries other than Canada are obliged to pay a fee for services at both the hospital and private medical clinics based on the type of treatment required. The fee could range from $30 for a simple consultation at a private clinic to $100 at a public clinic. Those unaccustomed to medicare may find they have more time to catch up on their reading in the waiting room than in a private clinic before seeing the doctor–**le médecin** or **le docteur** or the nurse–**l'infirmière** or **la garde-malade.** It's interesting to note in these days of sexual politics that **le médecin** is masculine and **la médicine** is the study of medicine. **L'infirmier(ière)** can be either masculine or feminine, but the person is often a female.

You will probably get treatment in the emergency clinic–**la clinique d'urgence,** or the local community health center–**le CLSC (Centre Local de Services**

Communautaires). Most CLSCs are staffed by doctors during the week, occasionally on weekends, rarely at night. The emergency health clinic is typically found in or near the hospital–**l'hôpital.** A teaching hospital is known as a **CHU–Centre Hospitalier Universitaire.**

AT THE HOSPITAL–À L'HÔPITAL

When you arrive at the hospital **réception**, you will be asked for your medicare card–**carte d'assurance-maladie.** If you need a wheelchair, ask for **le fauteuil roulant.** If you need to lie down you will be placed on a stretcher–**une civière** or in a hospital bed–**un lit.** All public buildings are accessible to handicapped persons, and other buildings with access ramps and facilities are indicated with a wheelchair pictogram.

If the doctor orders a blood test–**un test sanguin,** a nurse will take a blood sample–**une prise de sang.** If you're passed a small plastic bottle and asked for **un prélèvement d'urine,** pee in the bottle.

If you've had a ski or car accident you may be sent for an X-Ray–**une radiographie** and prescribed medication–**des médicaments** for pain. We hope you won't require a cast–**un plâtre** or stitches–**des points.** You may however experience pain–**la douleur.** To indicate where the pain is located simply point and say, **"J'ai mal . . ."** in the stomach–**au ventre,** in the back–**au dos,** in the ear–**à l'oreille,** in the throat–**à la gorge.** A headache is **un mal de tête,** a toothache is **un mal de dent.**

The doctor may tell you something is broken–**fracturé.** It may be a leg–**une jambe,** an arm–**un bras,** a finger–**un doigt,** your neck–**ton cou.** If you require crutches–**des béquilles,** they will be provided by the hospital or a pharmacy, usually for a small rental fee.

You could have an illness–**une maladie** or a discomfort–**un malaise.** If you have heart problems, use the word **cardiaque**—it sounds the same and works in both languages, as do **allergie** and **allergique.**

As in most of the rest of the world, AIDS is present in Quebec society, and the same letters are used to name the disease, but in a different order: **SIDA.** Sexually transmitted diseases are STDs in English, **MTS** (em-tay-ess) in French–**maladies transmises sexuellement.**

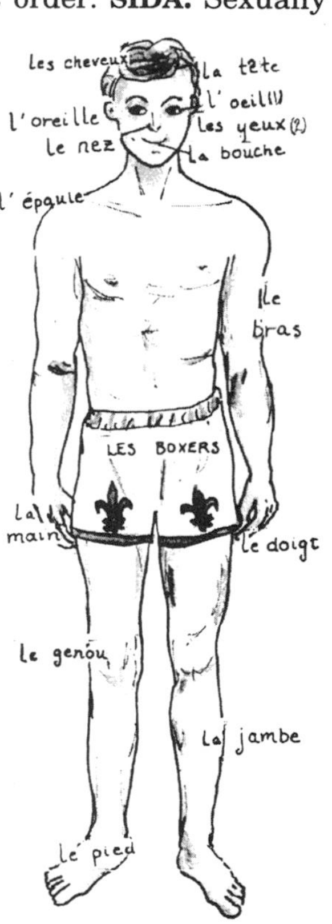

If you are pregnant–**enceinte** and your baby suddenly decides to become **un Québécois** or **une Québécoise,** your condition will be immediately obvious and it's unlikely you'll be doing much talking. The nurse may help you with your breathing–**respiration.** Breathe in–**aspirez;** blow out–**expirez.**

You may want to use the bedpan–**le bassin** or see the doctor–**je veux voir le médecin,** or leave–**je veux quitter** or **partir.** If you want to tell them you are in extreme pain and feel as if you've been run over by a train, groan loudly and say **mo-dee-sa-fa-mal!**

OTHER HEALTH–RELATED ITEMS

Some words sound the same in both languages but have different meanings. One hospitalized English-speaking woman provided her French-speaking nurse with more details than she needed to know when asked if she preferred to have her **douche** in the morning or at night. **Une douche** in French is a shower.

If you have lost your contact lenses: **"J'ai perdu mes lentilles cornéennes"** (lanh-tee-y' kor-nay-en) or **"mes verres de contact"** or glasses–**mes lunettes** or dentures–**mon dentier.**

In a city you can make an emergency call to **9-1-1.** Otherwise call the operator by dialing zero. In the front pages of the phone book a number of emergency numbers are listed. Many towns and cities also have a 24-hour emergency medical information phone line staffed by medical personnel to answer questions. The service is provided by the CLSC, and the number can usually be found in the phone book under **Centre Local de Services Communautaires.**

Stay healthy!

CHAPTER 8

INFORMATION PLEASE?

If you are into painting the town, it's important to know where to get the latest information on activities and events. Or if you can't start the day until you are up on the latest world happenings, you will be glad to know that most major Canadian and American daily newspapers make it to Montreal on the day they are printed, and the air waves enable Quebecers to receive all American television networks.

SOURCES OF INFORMATION

Les journaux are the daily newspapers, and **les hebdos** (from **hebdomadaire**, referring to a period of seven days) are published weekly. The main French-language dailies in Quebec are: in Montreal, the widely read **La Presse; Le Devoir,** which caters largely to academics and intellectuals; **Le Journal de Montréal,** which targets the masses—particularly sports fans and sensation-seekers—and in Québec city, **Le Soleil.** There are two English-language dailies: **The Gazette**, Montreal's only English-language daily, and **The Record**, published in Sherbrooke, a much smaller community-based daily serving the Eastern Townships. There are dozens of **hebdos** serving communities in French or English or both. Political analysts have a great time comparing the spin put on stories which appear on the front page of the Gazette with those on the front page, **la une,** of the French dailies.

While attending to domestic chores like doing the laundry–**faisant le lavage** or tidying up–**faisant le ménage** or just relaxing–**en détente,** you might want to tune in to a French-language radio or television station. **La Société Radio-Canada (SRC)** is the French-language version of the Canadian Broadcasting Corporation (CBC), and **Radio-Québec (RQ)** is the provincial sister. CTV–**TVA** and **Télévision Quatre-Saisons (TQS)** are commercial TV networks. Until you've mastered a fair bit of French, avoid the radio talk shows that combine passion and platitudes for a totally incomprehensible mix that might as well be coming from China or Japan.

There is a wonderful English-language FM radio service of the CBC called the Quebec Community Network, which brings local information as well as network programming to rural Quebec. The main news broadcasts picked up on CBC in Rivière-du-Loup or Iqualuit are the same as those heard all across Canada.

Many of the commercial TV programs on the French networks are dubbed versions of American shows, and even francophones are known to switch to an English channel rather than hear the lines after the actor has left the room. There are many French sitcoms–**les télé-romans,** almost all produced in Quebec, some of which, like soap operas, continue from week to week. They enjoy very large audiences.

Quebec has access to modern technology, and the American networks, weather channels, sports channels, music, all-news channels, e-mail and internet access (in cities and major towns) are available throughout the province.

LOOKING THINGS UP

It will be well worth your while to pay attention to details if you want to find the address or the phone number of the nice little restaurant you came across just after breakfast. Restaurants tend to have catchy names that start with **le** or **la,** and you may spend a considerable amount of time "letting your fingers do the walking". One thing you might remember is that most restaurants are listed under **Restaurant** in the white pages of the phone book, for example **Restaurant le Vieux Québec** or **Restaurant la Vieille Maison.** If, however, your restaurant decides to call itself simply **La Vieille Maison** you will have to check the phone book under **L.** The practice is to put abbreviations like **LMN Inc.** at the very beginning of the section of the alphabet, then all the places like **La Vieille Maison** before the words like **Labelle, Laboratoire,** and so on. It may take a bit of looking to find things that start with **l'** (ignore the apostrophe), **le** or **les,** like **L'Eau douce** or **le Vieux Québec** or **Les Anges.**

The **Saints** in the phone book may also give you a bit of trouble unless you realize that the abbreviation **St** is placed where "Saint" would be. For example, your friend is Joseph St-Laurent. To look up his name, look where s-a-i-n-t would be, near the beginning of the **S** section. (For a female saint, ignore the **e** of **sainte.**) Here's a list of things that are in alphabetical order as found in the Montreal phone book: Saigon, Sainsbury, Saint, St-Amand, Ste-Catherine, St-Laurent, St-Marc, Ste-Marie, St-Mark, St-Zotique, Sainville, Salon.

If looking for the name of a hotel or a hospital, check the phone book for **Hôtel** or **Hôpital.** The name of the place follows in French; for example, **Hôpital St-Luc, Hôtel Grand Central.** Similarly, **Garage** will often precede the owner's name, such as **Garage Jean-Noël.** It's sometimes very tricky, but if you remember little details like these, you should have no trouble finding information in various source books. For the Montreal phone book, you may also find a magnifying glass–**une loupe** useful!

Yellow pages–**les pages jaunes** do exist here. In Montreal and in some regions, there is an English section as well as a French section of **les pages jaunes.** The headings will be very useful. For example if you look up **Appliances–Major–Sales and Service,** you may be given the instruction: See also **Appareils électroménagers–Gros–Vente et service.** The ads in that section will most likely be bilingual.

SHOPPING

Logic—and a mean language deception—may tell you that **magasin** is a magazine and **librarie** is a library. Not so. A **magasin** is actually a store, and a magazine is **une revue. Librairies** are book stores, **papeteries** are office supply stores, and libraries (where you borrow books) are called **bibliothèques.** Most **bibliothèques** in Quebec offer a wide selection of both French and English books. A lecture is **un discours,** and **la lecture** is reading, with **un lecteur** being a male reader and **une lectrice** being of the female persuasion.

The main department stores–**les grands magasins** are Eaton (formerly Eaton's), La Baie (formerly Morgan's), Sears (formerly Simpson's), Zellers, Wal-Mart and just about any other major chains found throughout Canada. And of course there's Club Price which is Price Club everywhere else in Canada. If you plan to spend the day in the shopping mall–**le centre d'achat** or **centre commercial,** be sure to bring along your credit cards–**les cartes de crédit.** When you are ready to pay for your purchases, the clerk will likely ask you "cash or credit"–**"comptant ou carte de crédit?"** Credit card purchases benefit from the best foreign exchange rate, the one currently charged by banks.

Usually the sticker price is the price *before* taxes are added unless otherwise indicated. In Quebec, as in the rest of Canada, we have the Goods and Services tax (GST)–**Taxe sur Produits et Services (TPS)**, which is now 7 per cent and an additional 6.5 per cent Quebec sales tax (QST), **Taxe de Vente de Québec (TVQ).** So an item ticketed at $10.00 will have 7% **TPS** added to make it $10.70. The provincial **TVQ** of 6.5% is added to the $10.70 to make a total bill of $11.40. Some stores are trying to lessen the sting of the taxes and post signs indicating GST included–**TPS incluse** or All taxes included–**Toutes taxes incluses.** It's a good idea to have a pocket calculator with you for comparison shopping.

In addition to department stores and shopping malls, hundreds of boutiques specialize in clothing–**les vêtements,** toys–**les jouets,** shoes–**les chaussures.** A craft shop is **une boutique d'artisanat,** a gift shop is **une boutique de cadeaux,** and a duty-free shop–**une boutique hors taxes** is found in airports or at some Canada–U.S. border crossings. A jewellery store–**une bijouterie** sells jewels–**les bijoux.** A hardware store is **une quincaillerie.**

If you're looking for an everyday dress, you want **une robe,** but if you have a date for the New Year's Ball, you'll want **une robe de soirée** or **une tenue de soirée.** If you're buying a sweater–**un chandail** and pants–**un pantalon,** you might look for a jacket–**une veste** to make a complete outfit–**un ensemble.** A blouse is **un chemisier** or **une blouse** (pronounced blooz).

Other useful vocabulary:

washable–**lavable**
pure wool–**tout laine**
cotton–**le coton**
leather–**le cuir**
coat–**un manteau**
shirt–**une chemise**
socks–**des bas** or **des chaussettes**
stockings; panty-hose–**des bas; un bas-culotte**
tie–**une cravate**
shoes–**des souliers** or **des chaussures**
boots–**des bottes**
underwear–**des sous-vêtements**
size–**la pointure** (of shoe), **la taille** (of clothing)
length–**la longueur**
waist, belt–**la ceinture**

WHERE TO PURCHASE LIFE'S NECESSITIES

If you've been in Quebec more than 24 hours you must have concluded that **le dépanneur** (shortened to the depp) is that trusty corner store that's always there when you need it. **Dépanneurs** sell everything from tampons to beer and wine. The word **dépanneur** stems from the term **panne,** meaning something is missing or not working; and **un dépanneur** gets you out of your **pannes**—small ones you can buy your way out of anyway. **(Une panne d'électricité** is an electrical blackout.) Not all **dépanneurs** are as classy as the one in the picture opposite, but **le recyclage**–recycling even of old buildings is being done all over Quebec.

Weekly grocery shopping is often referred to as **faisant les emplettes.** To stock up on grocery supplies for the cottage or home you will visit the grocery store–**l'épicerie.** The larger Quebec chains are Richelieu, Provigo, Metro and IGA. Most grocery stores have an in-house

bakery–**une boulangerie,** a delicatessen–**une charcuterie,** and a butcher shop–**une boucherie.** You can pick up the catch of the day at **la poissonnerie** or at the wharf–**le quai** if you're anywhere near water. If you're travelling along **le St-Laurent** when fishermen are hauling in their nets, don't be too shy to stop by the wharf. They'll tell you a story in two languages about the one that got away.

You can buy beer–**la bière** and wine–**le vin** if you are over 18, the legal drinking age, at most **épiceries, dépanneurs,** and **supermarchés** until 11:00 P.M.–**23h.** To buy hard liquor–**l'alcool, les spiritueux,** and for an excellent selection of wines, you must go to a liquor store—**la Société des alcools,** which is indicated by a large squared white **Q** on a purple-red background. Some rural grocery stores are agents for **la Société des alcools** and carry **les spiritueux.** (All taxes are included in prices at a liquor store. Not so at the **dépanneurs,** where tax will be added to wine but not beer.) Soft drinks are called **boissons gazeuses** or

des liqueurs douces (a condemned anglicism). Most cans and bottles can be recycled, so you can return them to the seller to get your deposit back.

It should be mentioned that a dairy bar is **un comptoir laitier.** Milk–**lait** is sold in cartons–**des cartons** as well as in plastic bags–**des sacs en plastique.** Don't buy milk in bags unless you have the proper container for them.

A drug store is **une pharmacie.** Most drug stores in Quebec belong to chains, and you should look for the pharmacist's mortar and pestle symbol and a proper name followed by the inscription **pharmacien** or **pharmacienne.** The principal drugstore chains are Jean-Coutu, Pharmaprix, Obonsoins, Cumberland, Familiprix and Essaim. The stores sell everything from soup to nuts: toys, umbrellas, clothes, even prescription drugs.

A **tabagie** is a small store which sells newspapers, magazines, cigarettes, gum, toothpaste, and yes, condoms. Speaking of condoms, they are the same in both languages, and if the instructions on the package are written in French only, ask your partner for help.

OPENING HOURS–LES HEURES D'OUVERTURE

Catholic Quebec went the way of much of the rest of the world when it adopted laws allowing stores to open on Sundays. Most retail stores are open on Sundays, especially in tourist areas. They open around 10:00 or 11:00 **(10h, 11h)** in the morning and close at 5:00 **(17 heures)** or 6:00 **(18h)** except on Thursdays **(les jeudis)** and Fridays **(les vendredis)** when they may stay open to 9:00 **(21h).** Some small stores may be closed on Mondays **(les lundis)** and Tuesdays **(les mardis)** in the slow season. **Dépanneurs** are usually 7-11 stores **(7h-23h)** open seven days a week–**sept jours sur sept.**

ONE MAN'S GARBAGE IS ANOTHER MAN'S TREASURE

Bargain-hunters, write this one down: **un marché aux puces** is a flea market. If you plan to spend a lot of time in Quebec, this is a key phrase to learn. Once the snow vanishes, piles of rubble begin to appear in yards and roadsides everywhere with signs announcing **marché aux puces** or garage sale–**vente de garage.** This is a golden opportunity to buy that left Reebok you've always wanted or an ornamental electrical appliance. Shoppers have been known to walk away with could-a-been treasures, only to sell them a few weeks later at their own garage sale.

La pièce de résistance of Quebec bargain hunting is the auction–**l'encan,** a fascinating experience for novices who try to keep pace with a bilingual auctioneer taking bids on a bleating lamb or a color TV missing only the picture tube. Auctions are held in large halls in the cities and in tents in rural areas, when the weather is warm. They are more plentiful in spring and fall. If you think auctioneers are fast-talkers in one language, try making your bids when the patter is coming at you in two. You may walk away with a new pet.

WHERE TO LOOK FOR SERVICES

A post office is **un bureau de poste** (but it is a Canadian government service and is also allowed to call itself a post office). Feel free to invoke your right to speak English at this or any other *federal* institution. A mail box is **une boîte aux lettres.** Mail is **le courrier** and stamps are **les timbres.**

In 1996 it costs 45 cents plus GST and PST (add another 7 cents) to mail a letter or post card (under 30 grams in weight) to a Canadian destination and 52 cents plus GST and PST (8 cents tax) to mail a letter to the U.S.

Overseas mail costs double—90¢ + 12¢ tax. But if you mail something out of the country and the cost is over $5.00, there are no taxes to pay.

A customs office at the border of the country is called **les douanes.** This too is a federal institution, so customs officials are bilingual. An airport is **un aéroport,** a plane is **un avion**, a train station is **une gare de chemin de fer,** a bus station is **un terminus d'autobus,** a bus stop is **un arrêt d'autobus.** Departure times are indicated as **le départ** or just **Dép,** and arrival times are **l'arrivée** or **Arr**. Check *Getting there on time* in Chapter 10 for days of the week, months of the year and telling time. **Le Métro** in Montreal is the subway, but **la météo** is the weather forecast.

Let's hope you don't need medical services; but should you need a hospital it is indicated by a large **H** on a green background for **Hôpital** (pronounced oh-pee-tal). The emergency room is **la salle d'urgence.** You will easily recognize key words like **administration, ambulance,** and **réception.** A waiting room is **une salle d'attente.** Doctors are **médecins** or **docteurs,** medicine is **médicaments,** dentists are **dentistes,** nurses are **infirmières, gardes,** or **garde-malades.** More on health in Chapter 7 *On the Sidelines*.

Churches have services too, and a church is **une église.** United churches (which combine most small Protestant denominations) are **des églises unies,** Catholic churches are **des églises catholiques,** and Mass is **la messe.** Anglican (Episcopal) churches are **des églises anglicanes;** synagogues are **synagogues** in both languages. The priest is **le prêtre,** the minister is **le pasteur,** the rabbi is **le rabbin,** and the house of worship is **le lieu de culte.** The Catholic Church predominates in Quebec, and many noteworthy Stations of the Cross exist, some of which have been designed by great artists. Tourist guides may recommend **le Calvaire**–a wayside cross.

Car servicing is done in a garage or service center, pretty much the same in both languages: **le garage, le centre de service.** You buy gas at **un poste d'essence;** a self-serve pump is **auto-service** or sometimes **libre service.** Gas comes by the liter, and grades are bronze–**bronze**, silver–**argent,** or gold–**or,** with the most expensive being **en or.** There are 4.5 liters in an Imperial gallon, and 3.8 liters in an American gallon. Most service stations sell diesel fuel–**diesel** and propane–**gaz propane.** Lead-free gas is **sans plomb,** and all gas is lead-free. "Please check the oil"–**"Vérifiez l'huile, s'il vous plaît."**

PLACES TO GO

If you are going out for dinner (see Chapter 9 on food), you'll be looking for a restaurant. You might need **un téléphone** to make **des réservations** at the **théâtre** or the stadium–**le stade.** Admission–**Réseau Admission** is the place to buy your tickets for many concerts or sports events. Depending on the season, you may need a reservation at a country inn–**une auberge** or a Bed and Breakfast–**un gîte touristique** or **un gîte du passant.** If your resources are limited, a youth hostel–**une auberge de jeunesse** or a campground–**un terrain de camping** may be a better choice. You don't need reservations at **le bar** or **le disco** or the movie theatre–**le cinéma.** You can go to a pub–**une brasserie** and find some good inexpensive food along with the beer. The current show at the **théâtre** is what is **à l'affiche.**

On the marquee of the movie houses you may see beside the name of a movie the letters **VOA** or **VF.** Before the box-office hits make it to the English theatres, French versions must be available. It's hard to translate "Babe" or "Mary Reilly" into French, so before you walk into a theatre showing "Apollo 13", check to see if it is the original English version–**Version originale anglaise (VOA)** or the French version–**Version française (VF).** If you don't, you may hear something other than what you were expecting. Previews, however, may be in French at English movie houses.

The beach–**la plage** is a great spot to go in the summer. There are magnificent beaches on the Gaspé coast and along **le fleuve,** but the water is somewhat chilly. Freshwater lakes are numerous in Quebec, and most have excellent beaches.

In winter, head for the downhill ski center–**le centre de ski alpin** in the Laurentians–**les Laurentides,** the Eastern Townships–**l'Estrie** or **les cantons de l'Est,** and close by the Quebec city region–**la region de la ville de Québec.** The Gatineau region, north of Ottawa, in **l'Outaouais,** Charlevoix and Gaspé–**la Gaspésie** also have excellent downhill skiing. Rates are **les tarifs** and a special or package deal is **un for-fait!** You can find all the information you need on resorts in the provincial government tourist offices or in the copious information provided by Tourisme Québec (1-800-363-7777).

MONEY–LA MONNAIE, L'ARGENT

The Canadian dollar–**le dollar Canadien** is the unit of money used here. Commonly used bills–**les billets** are in denominations of five–**cinq,** ten–**dix,** 20–**vingt,** 50–**cinquante** and 100–**cent.** Commonly used coins–**les**

pièces or **de la monnaie** are in denominations of one cent–**un cent,** five cents–**cinq cents,** ten cents–**dix cents,** a quarter (twenty-five cents)–**un vingt-cinq cents** or **vingt-cinq cents,** one dollar–**un dollar** and two dollars–**deux dollars.** The dollar is a large gold-colored coin with a loon on it and is called a loonie–**un loonie** or **un huard.** A two-dollar coin featuring a polar bear–**un ours polaire** is the newest addition to our pocketbooks. The Canadian dollar is worth less than an American dollar, in recent years ranging from 72 to 86 cents U.S. Currently one Canadian dollar buys only 73 U.S. cents, and one U.S. dollar costs $1.37 Can. In larger centers, tourist areas or banks, the current exchange rate will be given on U.S. currency. In small towns you may have to dicker with the person you're doing business with.

WHEN YOU RUN OUT OF MONEY

A bank is **une banque.** Canada has six federally chartered banks: Royal Bank–**la Banque Royale,** Bank of Montreal–**la Banque de Montréal,** Bank of Nova Scotia–**la Banque de Nouvelle-Écosse (BNÉ),** Toronto-Dominion, the same in both languages **(TD),** National Bank of Canada–**la Banque Nationale,** and Canadian Imperial Bank of Commerce–**la Banque de Commerce (CIBC).** There are several credit unions, and the biggest is the **Caisse Populaire Desjardins** whose green and white logos can be found in almost every small town in Quebec. Most **Caisse Pops** are named for the parish or town they're in. They are affiliated with the big banks, and their automatic tellers work with most bank credit cards.

Banks are usually open from 10:00 to 3:00 **(10h–15h)** on weekdays, except Thursday or Friday when they may be open till 6:00 **(18h).** Only in major cities will any be open in the evenings or on Saturday. Debit cards are very popular here, and at any cash register even in small towns if you see signs "Direct Payment–**Paiement direct"** or "Interac", you can pay directly from your bank account or get cash advances.

Now here's a toughie, but you must remember it: an automatic teller, open 24 hours a day, is **un guichet automatique** or sometimes **des services automatisés.** The pictogram for this is a stylized calculator with or without a finger on it. Modern technology is wonderful, and usually if you have a bank card and insert it in the magic machine, it will ask you questions in the language in which the card is programmed. Or it may ask you if you would like to use English–**anglais** or French–**français.** If this doesn't happen, you might want to keep the following words in mind.

Punch in your personal identification number (your PIN number) if you see **Composez votre Numéro d'identification personnel (votre NIP).** A withdrawal is **un retrait** and a deposit is **un dépôt.** The amount is **le montant,** the balance is **le solde,** the drawer or place to put a deposit is **le tiroir** or maybe, if it slides, **le glissoir.** Chequing accounts show up as **épargne avec opérations** or **compte de chèques,** and a savings account is **épargne stable** or **compte d'épargne.** It seems that the programmers tried to use similar terms for both languages, and there may be a question like **Une autre transaction?** which means "Do you want to make another transaction?" Yes is **Oui** and No is **Non.** "Take the statement" is **prenez le relevé.** "Do you want an up-to-date statement?"–**une mise à jour?** on the screen?–**sur l'écran?** or a printout?–**ou imprimé?** Like a good machine, it will remind you to take your card at the end of it all with a message like **Prenez votre carte** or **N'oubliez pas votre carte.**

BUDGET TRAVEL TIPS

The best travel value is a package deal, which in Quebec is called **un forfait. Un prix forfaitaire**–a package deal price often includes activities, hotel room, and meals, so keep alert for this type of offer. You will find bargain rates in the off seasons, which are different in summer and winter. The slow times, especially in rural Quebec, are in May and June, and September and October. Great deals can be had on golf packages, cycling tours and all the rest. Early December, most of January, and early February are great times to get bargains on downhill skiing and other winter activities.

Dining out may be less romantic at mid-day, but the noon-time specials offer excellent choices and good value for your money. If you are in an area like downtown Montreal, your presence will bring more smiles if you arrive after 12:45, when the business crowd is heading back to the office towers.

Happy travelling! **Bon voyage!**

CHAPTER 9

FOODS FOR ALL SEASONS AND ALL TASTES

Synonymous with Quebecers' **joie de vivre** is their appreciation of fine foods and wines. Even a picnic is transformed into a party–**une fête** when locally grown fresh produce is teamed up with crusty breads–**les pains croûtés** from local bakeries–**les boulangeries locales,** cheeses–**les fromages,** and wines–**les vins,** from Quebec vineyards–**les vignobles.**

Eating is almost an obsession with Quebecers. In larger centers, you'll find restaurants catering to the most exotic tastes and featuring foods of every ethnic origin. But some of Quebec's greatest culinary treasures are hidden away, undiscovered except by locals and the intrepid who venture into tiny remote communities. The wharf-to-table seafood found on menus in **la Gaspésie** and **les Îles-de-la-Madeleine,** for example, cannot be matched anywhere in the world. From New York to Tokyo you may find Quebec produce in fine restaurants, perhaps Brome Lake Duck–**le canard du Lac Brome** or wild boar from Lac St. Jean–**du sanglier du Lac St-Jean.** Why not try them here?

EATING TRADITIONS

As Quebec becomes home to more and more immigrants, an increasing variety of ethnic foods can be found. There is a large Chinese community in Montreal, and both residents and visitors are frequently found in Chinatown on weekend mornings taking part in a ritual known as "dim sum", a veritable feast where waiters continuously roll in trays of food for visual as well as dining pleasure. A plethora of restaurants prepare authentic Greek and Italian foods reminiscent of the homeland, and eateries of all cultural persuasions line Duluth St. in central Montreal. Some even permit you to run next door to the local convenience store–**le dépanneur** to get a bottle of wine to go with dinner. Check for a sign in the window **"Apportez votre vin"** (B.Y.O.B., bring your own bottle of wine).

Another taste-treat to look for in Montreal is bagels—you can visit the Bagel Factory and watch bagels being baked before your eyes on rue St-Viateur near "The Main"–**rue St-Laurent.** It's been reported that chauffeur-driven limousines have been seen lining up after the theatre to allow well-heeled occupants to pick up fresh bagels for Sunday breakfast.

Montreal's reputation for smoked meat is legendary, and this is your opportunity to taste the real thing. Again, the **Office de la langue française** thinks you should order **"viande fumée",** but you're safe ordering **un smoked meat.** In Montreal, Ben's on De Maisonneuve, Dunn's on Ste-Catherine and Schwartz's (alias the Montreal Hebrew Delicatessen) on St-Laurent are the places to eat smoked meat, and all three are considered part of Montreal's "cultural experience".

Quebec City offers authentic French-Canadian fare in many of the delightful cafés and restaurants which line the cobblestone streets of Lower Town. In warm weather, evening dining at an outdoor **terrasse** is an experience not to be missed. Street musicians and performers, caricaturists, and artists line the streets while diners combine ambiance with some of the world's finest food.

If you venture outside the city to spend a day in the country, watch for church and community suppers where you'll find great home cooking. Establishments called **les tables champêtres** are usually open only in the evening with a limited choice of menu created from fresh local produce. Make a reservation and bring your own wine and a group of friends for good food at a reasonable price.

The larger cities and towns in "Mainland Quebec" will have a wide variety of eateries. In smaller towns, be forewarned that it may be hard to find a decent meal after 7 or 8 P.M. **(19 ou 20 heures).**

WHAT "REAL QUEBECERS" EAT

Quebec's popular claim to culinary fame is **poutine.** As mentioned earlier **poutine,** pronounced poo-teen, is very **québécois,** and even McDonald's, Burger King, and Wendy's have included it on their Quebec menus. Humpty Dumpty got into the act with poutine-flavored potato chips. What exactly is **poutine**? Essentially, it's a melange of French fries and cheese curds, topped with hot gravy. The best **poutines** are "discovered" at road-side canteens–**cantines** or **casse-croûte.**

Des casse-croûte are good sources of traditional fast foods. French fries are **frites,** and the portion–**le format** is small–**petit,** medium–**moyen** or large–**grand.** Onion rings are **rondelles d'oignon.** Hot dogs are very often **" 'ot dog",** and you can have them all dressed–**all dressed** or with mustard and relish–**avec moutarde et relish.** Here a gourmet fast food addict will almost always choose a **'ot dog stimé** over a **'ot dog grillé.** Hamburgers tend to be **" 'amburger"** regardless of what the language purists say. Cheeseburgers are just that, **les cheeseburgers.**

If you are fond of chicken the key word is **poulet,** and the two biggest places for **le poulet** are St. Hubert and **P.F.K. (Poulet Frit Kentucky),** the kind Colonel Sanders first licked from his fingers.

Not all foods have a distinct **québécois** character. A frequent snack anywhere recalls America's own May West, not the late movie queen, but the chocolate-covered sponge cake. It goes down well with **un Pepsi,** a popular soft drink in Quebec. Some Quebec employers eager to have a more health-conscious work force have replaced the traditional coffee break–**la pause café** with a health break–**une pause santé,** where the normal fare is juice–**du jus,** cheese–**du fromage,** and mineral water–**de l'eau de source.**

FOODS FOR ALL SEASONS

Food choices are both seasonal and regional. In the cold months of winter **la tourtière,** a ground pork pie, topped with a rich tomato relish or sauce, is a homey favorite frequently found on luncheon menus. **La tourtière** is also a requisite part of the traditional post-midnight mass celebration at Christmas, known as **le réveillon.** Pork and beans–**les fèves au lard,** pea soup–**la soupe aux pois,** and onion soup with cheese on top–**la soupe à l'oignon gratinée** rival other gourmet treats on a frosty winter evening. Stews–**des ragoûts** also chase away the winter chills.

La cuisine québécoise is often linked to the season and sport of the day. **Cipaille,** pronounced see-pie, is a wild game pie which originated in areas where hunting is popular.

A favorite winter sport in many areas of Quebec is ice-fishing–**la pêche sous la glace** or **la pêche blanche,** where whole families congregate in little shanties–**cabanes** on the ice. Most are equipped with pot-bellied stoves (Quebec heaters), and the devotees fish through holes drilled in the ice. The catch, which is tommycod in English, is called **les petits poissons des chenaux,** and is a local treat enjoyed in February or March.

In early March, the combination of mild days and cold nights provides ideal conditions to set the sap running in the abundant maple forests. It's sugaring-off time–**le temps des sucres.** There's usually still snow in the woods, but after a long cold winter it's a wonderful time all across the province. The farmers tap the maple trees in the sugar bush–**l'érablière,** and a pipe-line or buckets–**des seaux** are hung on each tap–**chaque entaille.** The sap–**l'eau** or **la sève** is collected and boiled for hours to concentrate the sweet syrup–**le sirop.** You can smell the sweetness in the air. A visit to a sugar shack–**une cabane à sucre** is a must.

There you can have an entire meal centered around maple syrup–**le sirop d'érable.** Usually there is ham–**le jambon,** scrambled eggs–**les oeufs brouillés,** crisp fried pieces of pork fat called **les oreilles-de-crisse,** sugar pie–**la tarte au sucre,** dumplings cooked in maple syrup–**les grands-pères** (no doubt a treat grandpa enjoyed and to which he gave his name), and most important of all **la tire sur la neige**–taffy on snow. **Tire** (rhymes with dear) is maple syrup boiled until thick then drizzled over snow to form a taffy which you roll on a popsicle stick. UM-M-M-M good! **C'est si bon!** Many sugar camps have sleigh rides–**les randonnées en traîneau** and other attractions as well.

The smelt–**l'éperlan** season begins around this time, and for some Quebecers it is a tradition to eat the tiny fish fried in bacon fat. Trout–**la truite** season opens around the end of April. Some of Quebec's best known rivers for fishing salmon–**le saumon** are found in the Gaspé and have provided sport and dinner for royalty and heads of state for years. The communities encircling the Gulf of the St. Lawrence river have some of the finest lobster–**le homard** and seafood–**les fruits de mer** to offer those venturing to Eastern Quebec.

FRESH FRUIT AND VEGETABLES

Another unique taste treat found in Quebec, this one in early May, is the fiddlehead fern–**les têtes de violon.** The not yet unfurled ferns collected on riverbanks are considered a delicacy when cooked, particularly when served with fresh salmon.

Asparagus–**les asperges** and rhubarb–**la rhubarbe** are the first fresh products to reach roadside fruit and vegetable stands–**les kiosques de fruits et de légumes.** Strawberries–**les fraises** are picked in late June, followed by raspberries–**les framboises,** then blueberries–**les bleuets.** In the Lac St-Jean area, the abundance of wild and cultivated blueberries has led to the locals being referred to as **les Bleuets.** The **Festival des Bleuets** is another occasion for celebration in late August. Many communities hold annual festivals promoting the specialties of their area. Festival queens have the dubious distinction of being crowned Strawberry Queen or Miss Salmon Festival.

Fresh corn–**le blé d'Inde** or **maïs** and tomatoes–**les tomates** are abundant in early August, and corn roasts–**les épluchettes de blé d'Inde** are very popular right through till early September. With September comes the apple harvest: among the many varieties grown in Quebec, the McIntosh is one of the finest eating apples found anywhere in the world. Apples–**les pommes** and fresh apple juice or cider–**le cidre** are available at all orchards–**les vergers.** Many orchards allow people to pick their own apples. Look for the roadside sign, U-pick–**Cueillez vous-mêmes.**

Vineyards–**les vignobles** are relatively new to Quebec and are enormously successful in the Eastern Townships and in Montérégie, where award-winning wines are produced. Most of the vineyards offer guided tours and wine-tasting. If you like what you taste, buy it on the spot. You won't find locally produced wines on many menus, at the corner store–**le dépanneur** or at the local **Société des alcools,** one reason being that they are not produced in large quantities.

Most areas of Quebec have 100 frost-free growing days (some microclimates have a slightly longer growing season). In the countryside it's fun to watch the haying (hay is **le foin),** which takes place from June through August. Most farmers get one or at most two hay crops.

In Montreal, you can plant your tomatoes at the end of May, but in the rural areas those tender crops are not usually planted in gardens until early June. Outside the cities the last spring frost–**le dernier gel** is in early June, and by the end of August gardeners are wary of the first fall frost.

FALL AND THE HARVEST–L'AUTOMNE ET LA RÉCOLTE

Harvest begins in early September, and the root crops are dug out of the ground by the end of the month. Those maple trees, so generous with their sap early in the year, start to change color in mid-August, signalling the beginning of the harvest–**la récolte.** The beautiful fall colors reach their peak in mid to late September and are still brilliant in the first week of October.

Maple leaves are **les feuilles d'érable.** They come in brilliant shades of red–**rouge** and yellow–**jaune.** A light coat of paraffin wax or pressing them in a heavy book will preserve the colors nicely if you want to show them to faraway friends or relations.

Fall also brings the hunting season. Small game is called **gibier,** but the serious outdoorsman heads north to hunt moose–**l'orignal** or a little later will go after deer–**le chevreuil** in southern Quebec. In Quebec's deer hunting season (end of October to mid-November) it is wise to wear very bright colors when taking a walk along country roads or in the woods (perhaps even wiser to stay out of the woods).

DINING OUT

Quality restaurants abound in Quebec, and Quebecers make it a habit to dine out often. The cuisine varies with the region. Literally translated, **une cuisine** means a kitchen, but the word is also used to define a style of cooking. Quebec chefs are creative, and each chef has his or her own specialties. Culinary experiments frequently appear on the menu of the day–**la table d'hôte,** which is often the most economical way of eating out. **La table d'hôte** usually features an appetizer–**un hors d'oeuvre** or **une entrée,** a soup–**une soupe** or **un potage,** the main dish–**le plat principal,** and a dessert–**un dessert.** A beverage–**un breuvage** is also included for one fixed price. If **la table d'hôte** doesn't appeal to you, you can order from the menu **à la carte.**

HERE WE TAX THE TAX

Don't forget that unless specified the GST (Goods and Services Tax)–**la TPS (la Taxe sur Produits et Services)** of 7% and the PST (Provincial Sales Tax)–**la TVQ (la Taxe de Vente du Québec),** an additional 6.5%, will also be added to the total bill. If there is an indication on the bill that **Service** (15%) has also been added, don't leave a tip. Tips are usually calculated at 10 to 15% of the bill *before* taxes are added.

U.S. tourists may qualify for GST **(TPS)** rebates. Keep your receipts and ask at the customs office–**les douanes.**

A VERY NICE SIGN–OUTSIDE

It can be embarrassing to go into a restaurant, get nicely settled, study the menu and realize that either your taste buds or your pocketbook are not quite prepared for this dining experience. Fortunately, Quebec eating establishments post their menus outside. You may have rain drizzling down your neck as you check the fare, but you will have an excellent idea of how much you will shell out at the end of the evening. **Le menu est affiché à l'extérieur du restaurant**–the menu is posted outside the restaurant.

When you enter a restaurant, you may see a sign saying **Attendez l'hôtesse s.v.p.**–Please wait for the hostess to seat you. Your hostess–**votre hôtesse** will ask if you'd like to be seated in an area reserved for smokers or non-smokers–**section fumeur ou non-fumeur.** Many restaurants have bilingual menus, but your dining experience will be enhanced if you successfully order in French, so give it a try.

If you're ordering steak–**du steak,** well-done is **bien-cuit,** medium is **medium,** and rare is **saignant.** The waitress may ask if you would like your potato baked–**patate au four** or **pomme de terre au four,** mashed–**patates pilées,** or fried–**frites.** If you have a complaint–**une plainte** about the cold soup, ask the waitress to warm it up: **réchauffez, s'il-vous-plaît.** If you want the service to speed up, tell the waitress you're in a hurry, **je suis pressé.**

Wine is **le vin,** white wine is **le vin blanc,** and red wine **le vin rouge.** In addition to an extensive wine list, most restaurants have a cheaper but decent house wine–**un vin maison,** which comes in quantities of a half liter–**un demi-litre,** a quarter liter–**un quart de litre** or a liter–**une carafe** or **un litre.**

As you enjoy your meal, the waitress may stop to ask if the meal is satisfactory: **Est-ce que c'est à votre goût?** If it is, Yes, thank you–**oui, merci** is the only response necessary. If you want to get into the specifics, you're on your own.

Since your objective is to enjoy your dining experience and not necessarily to maintain the purity of the French language, it's quite acceptable to use a mixture of French and English words and phrases, along with a smile–**un sourire** in order to be understood.

SOME USEFUL FOOD-RELATED VOCABULARY

addition, l'	the bill
à la carte	regular menu
assiette, une	plate or platter
beurre, le	butter
beurre d'arachides	peanut butter
brasserie, la	pub, for beer and inexpensive meals
café, le; un café	coffee; coffee shop
caisse, la	the cash
caissier, -ière	the cashier
carte de crédit, la	credit card
champignons, les	mushrooms
combien?	how much?
comptant	cash
comptoir, le	counter
confiture, la	jam
couteau, un	knife
cuillère, la	spoon
crêpes, des	pancakes or crepes
crevettes, des	shrimp
cuisine minceur	low-calorie cooking
cuisine végétarienne	vegetarian cuisine
déjeuner, le	breakfast
dessert, le	dessert in both languages
dîner, le	lunch or dinner at noon
entrecôte, une	steak
entrées, les	appetizers (not the main dish)
épices; épicé	spices; spicy
fines herbes, les	herbs used in cooking
fourchette, la	fork
fruits de mer, les	sea food
gourmet, un	someone knowledgeable about food and wine
gourmand, un	a person fond of eating

haute cuisine, la	fine dining
homard, le	lobster
hors-d'oeuvres	appetizers
huîtres, les	oysters
jus, le; du jus d'orange	juice; orange juice
légumes, les	vegetables
miel, le	honey
moutarde, la	mustard
pain, le	bread
pain blanc, le	white bread
pain de blé entier, le	whole wheat bread
pâté, le (paw-tay)	a spread of finely chopped or pureed meat
pâtes, les (pawt)	pasta
petits pains, les	rolls
pétoncles, les	scallops
plat principal, le	the main dish
poivre, le	pepper
pommes de terre, les or **patates, les**	potatoes
potage, le; la soupe	soup
poulet, le; une poitrine; une cuisse	chicken; breast; leg
pourboire, un	(literally "for drink") tip
repas, le	meal
salades, les	salads
salle à manger, la	dining room
sel, le	salt
serviette, une	napkin
souper, le	supper
table d'hôte, la	complete meal specials
thé, le	tea
tisane, une	herbal tea
verre, le; verre d'eau	glass; glass of water

Bon appétit! Enjoy your meal!

CHAPTER 10

RECREATION, SPORTS AND EVENTS

Once upon a time Quebec was described by Voltaire as "A few acres of snow"–**"Quelques arpents de neige".** More recently the great French Canadian singer-poet Gilles Vigneault wrote a popular song **"Mon pays, ce n'est pas un pays, c'est l'hiver!"**–My country isn't a country, it's winter! These two gentlemen may have exaggerated somewhat, but when it isn't winter, Quebecers go frantic with outdoor activities from May–**mai** till October–**octobre.** Then the sport which consumes most **Québécois** takes over: hockey–**le hockey.**

HOCKEY–LE HOCKEY

Kids play street hockey spring and fall, older folks watch hockey and the playoffs right through until June–**juin.** There is no doubt that it is the dominant sport in Quebec. Hockey is played primarily by men, but more and more women are taking up the sport. There are leagues for "old timers" and pick-up games at ice rinks all over the province. Arenas are rented out by the hour, and some are open all night to accommodate the needs of hockey players of all shapes and sizes.

Le hockey is helped by the fact that Montreal has one of the original six franchises in the National Hockey League (NHL)–**la Ligue Nationale de Hockey (LNH).**

Les Canadiens have long been rivals of **les Maple Leafs** of Toronto. **Les Canadiens** or the Habs (from **"les Habitants",** the French settlers in rural Quebec) used to play at the Forum–**le Forum** in the west central area of Montreal. In March, 1996 they moved to a new facility closer to downtown: the Molson Center–**le Centre Molson.** Fans of **les Canadiens** in Montreal are highly knowledgeable about the game, and they keenly appreciate skilled play.

Quebec City recently said adieu to its NHL franchise–**les Nordiques,** as they headed to Denver to become the Avalanche. There never was a greater rivalry than that between **les Nordiques** and **les Habs,** and hockey fans will miss it.

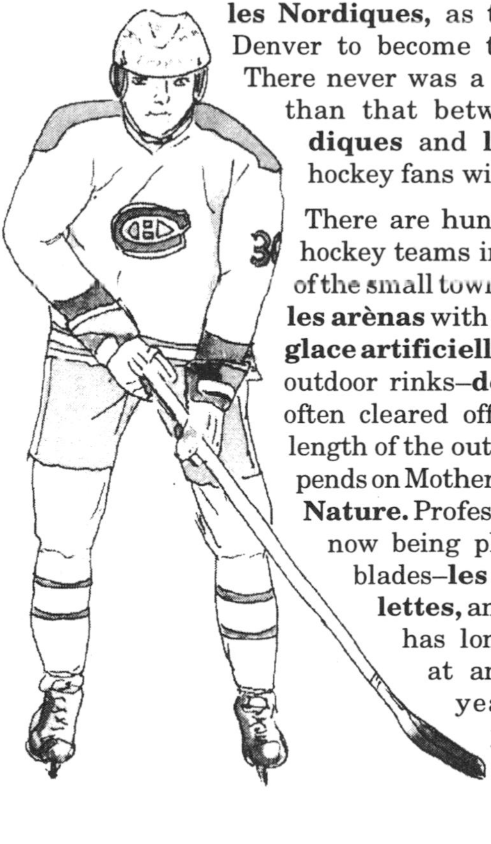

There are hundreds of junior hockey teams in Québec. Most of the small towns have arenas–**les arènas** with artificial ice–**la glace artificielle.** Villages have outdoor rinks–**des patinoires,** often cleared off by hand. The length of the outdoor season depends on Mother Nature–**Dame Nature.** Professional hockey is now being played on roller blades–**les patins à roulettes,** and street hockey has long been played at any time of the year by most young Quebecers.

Here's some of the hockey jargon: skates–**les patins,** the net–**le filet,** the puck–**la rondelle,** the stick–**le bâton,** the helmet–**le casque,** a goal–**un but,** the game–**le jeu,** the players–**les joueurs,** the goalie–**le gardien,** the forwards–**les attaquants,** the defencemen–**les défenseurs,** the centre–**le joueur de centre,** the right wing–**l'ailier droit,** the left wing–**l'ailier gauche,** the referees–**les arbitres.** He shoots, he scores! **Il lance, il compte!**

BASEBALL–LE BASE-BALL

There is another professional team of note in Quebec: the baseball team–**l'équipe de base-ball** named the Montreal Expos– **les Expos de Montréal.** The Expos play in the National League–**la ligue Nationale,** and their home park is the Olympic Stadium–**la Stade Olympique** in east-end Montreal. The Olympic Stadium, built for the 1976 summer Olympics, is round and is more or less affectionately dubbed the Big Owe because of the huge debt incurred in constructing it and its costly roof.

Some baseball terms: the pitcher–**le lanceur,** the catcher–**le receveur,** first base–**le premier-but,** second base–**le deuxième-but,** third base–**le troisième-but,** short stop–**l'arrêt-court,** infield–**l'avant-champ,** outfield–**l'arrière-champ,** at bat–**au bâton,** ball–**balle,** strike–**prise,** out–**retiré,** safe–**sauf,** stolen base–**but volé,** a hit–**un coup sur,** a home run–**un circuit,** a grand slam–**un grand chelem,** an inning–**une manche.**

Montreal has a professional soccer team, the Impact, which many hope will have an impact on the fans. And after many years, Alouettes will again be playing Canadian football for Montreal.

OLYMPICS–LES OLYMPIQUES

Montreal was the site of the 1976 summer Olympics, and Quebec City was one of the final four competing for the winter games of 2002. Quebec has produced some outstanding Olympians. Recent heroes include Myriam Bédard with two gold medals in the biathlon, Jean-Pierre Brassard with gold in moguls freestyle skiing, Sylvie Fréchette with gold in synchronized swimming, and Sylvie Bernier and Anne Montminy, champion divers.

Then there are the skaters: Gaetan Boucher, an outstanding speed skater; Sylvie Daigle, Natalie Lambert, Frédéric Blackburn, short track speed skaters; Sylvain Bouchard, who broke the world record for speed skating in 1995, though not an Olympian; Isabelle Brasseur and Lloyd Eisler, world champion pairs skaters, Josée Chouinard, and many more.

OUTDOOR SPORTS

Other sports played outside–**à l'extérieur** include soccer–**le soccer,** tennis–**le tennis** and golf–**le golf.** In summer, **en été,** Quebecers who like the water also go canoeing, boating or sailing–**on fait du canot, du bateau ou de la voile.**

Sports-minded folks or athletes swim, dive, run and cycle–**les sportifs ou les athlètes font de la natation, de la plongée, de la course à pied et du vélo (ou du cyclisme).** A swimmer is **un nageur** or **une nageuse,** a runner is **un coureur** or **une coureuse,** a cyclist is **un(e) cycliste.** A sailor is **un marin** or **un matelot,** a sailboat is **une voilier,** a canoe is **un canot,** a kayak is **un kayak,** a motorboat is **un bateau à moteur** or **un hors-bord,** a paddle or an oar is **un aviron** or **une rame,** a sail is **une voile.** Some resorts or cottagers have little paddleboats called **les pédalos.**

A swimming pool is **une piscine,** a bicycle path is **une piste cyclable,** and a hiking trail is **un sentier pédestre.**

GOLF–LE GOLF

Here the season is short, from mid-May to mid-October, depending on the weather of course. Since much of North America has gone golf-crazy it's important to know some of the approved golf terms. Golfers are **des golfeurs** or **golfeuses,** the course is **le terrain de golf.** Other terms used in this sport are: the fairway–**l'allée,** the rough–**l'herbe longue,** the woods–**les bois,** the sand trap–**le fosse de sable,** the tee–**le tertre de départ,** the green–**le vert.**

The wooden tee is **le té,** the clubs are **les bâtons,** a wood being **un bois,** an iron–**un fer,** a putter–**un putter** or **un fer droit.** The ball is **la balle** or **le ballon.** The score is **le compte,** par is **la normale,** a birdie is **un birdie** or **un oiselet,** bogey is **un bogey** and an eagle is **l'aigle.** Most players will get out of your way if you yell "Fore!"

INDOOR SPORTS AND OTHER SPORTS TERMINOLOGY

Sports often played in a gym–**un gymnase** or on a special court include volleyball–**le volleyball,** badminton–**le badminton,** squash–**le squash** and basketball–**le basket** (invented and first played in Montreal).

A racket is **une raquette (des raquettes** are snowshoes, not an indoor sport!), the ball is **la balle,** the birdie or shuttlecock is **l'oiseau,** the net is **le filet,** the court is **le court,** the score is **le compte,** the winner is **le gagnant,** the loser is **le perdant,** and a tie is **l'égalité.** Players are **les joueurs,** a game is **un match** or **une partie,** and sports events between teams are **les matchs.**

WINTER SPORTS–LES SPORTS D'HIVER

Some winter sports–**quelques sports d'hiver** besides **le hockey** are: skating–**le patinage,** figure skating–**le patinage artistique,** speed skating–**le patinage de vitesse;** ice fishing is **la pêche sur glace** or **la pêche blanche;** curling is **le curling;** sliding is **glisser,** and slides are **des glissades;** downhill skiing is **le ski alpin,** cross-country skiing is **le ski de fond;** snow-shoeing is **faire de la raquette,** walking is **la marche.** Trails are **des sentiers,** climbing is **l'escalade.**

If you are a lover of alpine skiing–**le ski alpin,** you should know that bindings are **les attaches,** boots are **des bottes,** poles are **des bâtons,** skis are **les skis,** and the tips of the skis are **les spatules.** A chair lift is **un remonte-pente,** slopes are **les pentes,** and at the top of the lifts there is often a unilingual French sign which says **Préparez-vous à descendre**–Prepare to get off, or **Levez les spatules**–Lift your ski tips. The ski patrol–**les patrouilleurs** will come to your aid if necessary. For some, the pleasantest part of downhill skiing is the camaraderie in the **auberge** that comes afterwards, **l'après-ski.**

LEISURE ACTIVITIES–LES LOISIRS

Other leisure activities–**des loisirs** or pastimes–**des passe-temps** include playing cards–**jouer aux cartes,** chess–**aux échecs,** bridge–**au bridge,** solving puzzles–**les casse-tête,** chatting–**causer** or **jaser,** reading–**la lecture** or **lire,** or just hanging out–**flâner.**

We can't forget bird watching–**l'observation des oiseaux,** whale watching–**l'observation des baleines,** hiking–**la randonnée pédestre,** sightseeing–**visites des monuments,** or **promenades en voiture,** guided tours–**visites guidées,** and shopping–**le magasinage.**

Nevada North has gone bonkers over casinos, and there are casinos in Montreal, in Charlevoix at La Malbaie and a new one opening in Hull. The dealer is **le croupier,** and he deals from the shoe–**le sabot.** He will ask you to place your bets–**faire vos jeux.** When the betting is closed he will say, **"Rien ne va plus."** The deal is **la donne,** the hand is **la main,** bets are **les mises,** and for more money you may have to go to **la banque.**

Chips are **les jetons,** slot machines are **les machines à sous.** If you are gambling, you are playing **les jeux de hasard.** Horse racing is carried on at **le hippodrome,** where the pari-mutuel betting windows will take your money; then you can take in the races–**les courses de chevaux.**

HUNTING AND FISHING–LA CHASSE ET LA PÊCHE

The hunting and fishing riches of this rugged landscape have for a long time attracted kings and presidents, and hundreds of thousands of sportsmen from far and wide. In the last few years, communing with nature has become popular. Modern technology has seen the invention of fabrics and outdoor equipment that allow those interested to take to the great outdoors looking for relaxation or excitement in ever-increasing numbers.

Quebec's parks and wildlife reserves–**les réserves fauniques** allow you to relax in the fresh air and enjoy activities such as backpacking, hiking, rock climbing, mountain biking, rafting, canoeing, whale watching, fishing and wildlife observation or hunting.

The multitudinous rivers and lakes in Quebec are usually open to anglers–**les pêcheurs** from late April to the fall. Fishing permits, available in sporting goods stores, are required. They are issued for periods of three days to a full season, depending on species. And don't forget, in the winter we also go ice fishing–**la pêche blanche.**

Hunting–**la chasse** is a fall and winter sport. Again permits are necessary. Years ago there was a vast number of private hunting and fishing clubs across the province. To allow all sportsmen to have equal access to these territories controlled by licenced associations, the government opened the clubs as controlled public hunting and fishing areas–**les zones d'exploitation contrôlée (ZECs).** In addition the government created a number of wildlife reserves–**les réserves fauniques,** where the luck of the draw determines who can hunt what and when. In the more populated areas of the province, land is clubbed, and local game wardens police it to ensure the club rules are respected. Outfitters–**les pourvoiries** offer lodging and all services necessary for those who want to enjoy hunting and fishing and outdoor activity.

FESTIVALS

There are surely as many festivals–**les festivals** as there are days in the year in Québec. In February–**février** every town and village has a carnival–**carnaval,** but undoubtedly **la ville du Québec** hosts the best known winter carnival around.

When all Catholics went to church, the Lenten season–**le Carème** which precedes Easter–**Pâques** was a quiet time, and the **Carnaval de Québec** ends just before Lent begins. Shrove Tuesday–**Mardi Gras** (Fat Tuesday) is the day before Ash Wednesday–**le mercredi des Cendres,** and **Mardi Gras** is party time in Quebec as well as in Rio and New Orleans.

Sports festivals, ski races, cross-country ski marathons, snowmobile treks and numerous other events provide distractions during those long months to stave off cabin fever. In summer it's on to another orgy of outdoor festivals, concerts, fireworks displays, regattas, bicycle, car and foot races. Quebecers like lots of distractions. Politics–**la politique** is a sport here too, 10 months a year (even politicians like to take the summer off).

CALENDAR INFORMATION

The months of the year–**les mois de l'année** are fairly close to those in English, as are their abbreviations:

January–**janvier (jan)**
February–**février (fév)**
March–**mars**
April–**avril**
May–**mai**
June–**juin**
July–**juillet (juil)**
August–**août**
September–**septembre (sept)**
October–**octobre (oct)**
November–**novembre (nov)**
December–**décembre(déc)**

The days of the week are hard to remember because there are no real memory hooks. **Mardi** in **Mardi Gras** is Tuesday as in Shrove Tuesday, Saturday starts with **S** in French and in English, and that's about as close a hook as you can find. The days are all masculine. Wednesday is the longest weekday name in English, in French, Friday–**le vendredi** is as long as **le mercredi.** Here they are: the days of the week. **Les voici: les jours de la semaine.**

Monday–**le lundi (lun)**
Tuesday–**le mardi (mar)**
Wednesday–**le mercredi (mer)**
Thursday–**le jeudi (jeu)**
Friday–**le vendredi (ven)**

The weekend–**la fin de semaine** or **le weekend** consists of Saturday–**le samedi (sam)** and Sunday–**le dimanche (dim).**

DURING THE DAY

Mornings are **les matins,** so Tuesday morning is **le mardi matin,** noon is **midi,** afternoon is logically **après-midi;** and Sunday afternoon is **le dimanche après-midi.** Evenings are **les soirs;** Friday night is **le vendredi soir.** Midnight is **minuit.**

In English, folks often say "Have a good day!" when saying goodbye to a friend. The French language has a much simpler way of saluting people. **Bonjour!** is Hello or Good day! **Bonne journée!** means "Have a good day" all day long. Similarly you hear **Bonne soirée**–Have a good evening, **Bonne nuit**–Good night, and **Bonne Année**–Happy New Year!

Most people go to bed at night–**on se couche le soir** and get up in the morning–**on se lève le matin.** An early riser is called **un lève-tôt.** A nap in the afternoon is **un petit somme l'après-midi** and a siesta, **une sieste.** Breakfast is **le déjeuner,** lunch–**le lunch** or **le dîner,** and dinner–**le souper.** A snack–**un goûter** is fine any time of the day.

COUNTING THE HOURS AND OTHER NUMBERS

The hours of the day–**les heures de la journée:**

1 un, **2 deux,**
3 trois, **4 quatre,**
5 cinq, **6 six,**
7 sept, **8 huit,**
9 neuf, **10 dix,**
11 onze, **12 douze (midi),**
13 treize, **14 quatorze,**
15 quinze, **16 seize,**
17 dix-sept, **18 dix-huit,**
19 dix-neuf, **20 vingt,**
21 vingt et un, **22 vingt-deux,**
23 vingt-trois and **24 vingt-quatre (minuit).**

Even numbers are **chiffres pairs,** and odd numbers are **chiffres impairs.**

The key hours to remember are 6:00 P.M.–**18 h.** to 8:00 P.M–**20 h.,** if you are going to meetings and such. 8:15 is **huit heures quinze le matin** or **huit heures et quart.** On the dot: 10 o'clock on the dot or 10 o'clock sharp is **dix heures pile.** 9:30 A.M. is **neuf heures trente** or **neuf heures et demie.** 2145 is **vingt et une heures quarante-cinq** or **vingt-deux heures moins quinze,** and in the rest of North America it's 9:45 P.M.

Other numbers worth remembering are:

50 cinquante,
75 soixante-quinze,
80 quatre-vingts,
90 quatre-vingt dix,
100 cent,
500 cinq cents and
1000 mille.

HOLIDAYS

A holiday is **un congé,** vacations are **des vacances,** and a legal holiday is often referred to as **un jour férié.** Major legal holidays when banks and almost everything else is closed are:

January 1, New Year's Day–**le Jour de l'An**
Good Friday–**le Vendredi Saint**
Easter Monday–**le lundi de Pâques**
Victoria Day in English Canada–**la Fête de Dollard** in Quebec (the second to last Monday in May)
June 24–**la St-Jean-Baptiste,** Quebec's National Holiday–**la Fête nationale du Québec**
July 1, Canada Day–**la Fête du Canada**
Labor Day–**la Fête du Travail,** the first Monday in September
Thanksgiving Day–**le Jour de l'Action de Grâce,** the second Monday in October
December 25, Christmas–**Noël**

Quebec has distinctly North American habits, and we celebrate things like Valentine's Day–**la St-Valentin,** St. Patrick's Day–**la St-Patrick,** Easter–**Pâques,** Mother's Day–**la Fête des Mères,** Father's Day–**la Fête des Pères,** Halloween–**l'Halloween,** Remembrance Day–**le Jour du Souvenir,** Boxing Day–**le lendemain de Noël.**

Quebec has an inexplicable custom of ending most residential leases on June 30. School is out, and so it seems most people choose to move at this time of the year. While this choice avoids the problems of moving in a snowstorm, it does create great difficulty in hiring either a truck or a moving company. So try not to meet the thousands doing their best to get the sofa into Dad's car as they move from one living space to another on July 1, when most sane people are out enjoying splendid weather and the Canada Day holiday.

There are two very busy holiday periods when tourist spots will be excessively busy. The first is the "construction holidays" which fall in the last two full weeks of July. Not only are construction workers on holiday, many factories close down too. The other busy period is between Christmas and New Year's Day, when many offices close for the week. Public schools have a week-long shutdown in late February or early March. However, each school board chooses its holiday period, and the entire province does not shut down the same week.

You have been warned that Quebecers love to party, so on long holiday weekends you will find lots of activities scheduled all over Quebec. It's worth taking time to enjoy some of them—but book early!

EPILOGUE

QUEBEC: Bonjour, eh? has had a long gestation period. The idea was conceived following the adoption of Bill 178, a law banning languages other than French on commercial signs, and its birth follows the referendum of October 30, 1995.

As moderate long-time activists in Quebec's English-speaking community, we feel that at this time in the history of Quebec and Canada our governments should be looking at the real problems facing each of us: education, health care, environment, job creation, care of the elderly, sharing our wealth. . . . We also believe that Canadians as individuals should be putting a great deal more effort into getting to know one another.

Quebec is our homeland–**notre patrie**. All ten of our children were raised here, and, like millions of other **Québécois,** we have tangled roots. There's Irish, Scotch, French, Indian, and British blood coursing in our veins. We don't think it matters a bit what percentage is more significant. We consider ourselves **Québécoises.**

Consider the story of the young Irish lad Tec Nil Aubry, orphaned on his arrival in Canada, who was taken in by a French-Canadian family. When he was about to be married, the parish priest went to great lengths to find the young man's birth certificate only to discover that

Tec Nil Aubry had been baptised Teague Cornelius O'Brennan and had not a drop of French blood in his veins!

And then there's the story of a distant relative named Ursule Gervais, born in Montreal, married and died in Ontario. One of her descendants surnamed Clairmont was doing research on his family tree and came upon information about the family patriarch, who had been a Clermont from Quebec. He also discovered that Ursule Gervais had been transformed for a time into Ursula Jarvis. A real Quebecer? Who's to say?

Quebecers and other Canadians have much in common. The view that some Canadians have of Quebecers might change dramatically if they came here to meet and greet some of their distant cousins.

Similarly some Quebecers assume that the vast majority of English-speaking people of this country automatically oppose all of Quebec's claims and are almost totally ignorant of Quebec's concerns. In an editorial titled **No time to trade historical shots** printed in *The Record* of September 14, 1992, Sharon wrote:

> But what do Quebecers know of the aspirations of Western Canadians? Do they empathize with their compatriots in Newfoundland over the closure of the fishery? Have they ever experienced a prairie winter or studied wheat prices in their daily newspaper? What do any of us know about the dreams and aspirations of native peoples?
>
> The vast geography of this country, its two languages, and the parochial, provincial and selective view of history taught in Canadian classrooms have all contributed to the lack of understanding.
>
> While it may be true that many English-speaking Canadians don't know that it was the

French explorers Joliet, Marquette, LaSalle and La Vérendrye who settled the territory from Lake Winnipeg to the Rockies, it's usually left unstated that they were met by natives. And naturally, Quebec's demands for special status would seem offensive to those unaware of its historic struggle for recognition.

As far back as 1822, Louis-Joseph Papineau described Lower Canada (Quebec) as "a distinct geographic, economic and cultural space, forever destined to serve the 'habitant' as a Catholic and French nation."

But that's all history. And unless the past is used as a springboard to something bigger and better, it's best left gathering dust in a library. Certainly this is not the time to drag it out and start trading historical shots like, "I'll give you two Durhams for one conscription, one Brockville flag stomper for three **arrêt** signs, an expulsion for an exodus."

In spite of our historical warts, we have managed to build a country to be proud of—a 125-year-old nation with two official languages, many cultures and the highest standard of living in the world.

At the end of your sojourn we hope you will be able to say, “We think we understand. This is a special place!”

THE MOMS' LITTLE DICTIONARY

FRENCH TO ENGLISH

There are several specialized vocabularies in the text:

aéroport, un–airport
affiche, une; à l'affiche–poster; what is playing at a theatre or movie house
âge d'or, personne agée (fem.)–senior citizen
air climatisé, l' (masc.), **l'air conditionné**–air conditioning
Amusez-vous bien!–Enjoy yourself!
anglais, l' (masc.), **la langue anglaise**–the English language
anglophone, l' (masc., fem.)–anglophone, an English-speaking person
année, l' (fem.); **Bonne Année!**–year; Happy New Year

après; l'après-midi (masc. or fem.)–after; afternoon
argent, l' (masc.); **monnaie, la**–silver, money; change (coins)
arrêt, un; un arrêt d'autobus; un arrêt-court–stop, a stop; bus stop; short stop (in baseball)
arrière, derrière–back, behind
arrivée, l' (fem.)–arrival, arrival time
ascenseur, l' (masc.)–elevator
assez–enough
Attendez le signal–Wait for the signal
Au revoir!–Good bye! Till we meet again!
auberge, l' (fem.); **auberge de jeunesse**–inn, country inn, small hotel; youth hostel
aujourd'hui–today
auto, l' (fem.), **la voiture**–car, automobile
auto-service, l' (masc.), **service libre**–self-serve (at a garage)
auto-stop, l' (masc.), **faire du pouce**–hitchhike
automne, l' (masc.)–autumn
autoroute, l' (masc.)–expressway, limited-access highway
avant–before
avion, un–airplane
avoir: j'ai, tu as, il a, nous avons, vouz avez, ils ont–to have: I have, you have (sing.), he has, we have, you have (pl.), they have
bain, le; la salle de bain; la toilette–bath; bathroom; toilet
baleine, la–whale
banlieue, la–suburb, outskirts of a city
bas, basse; le Bas Canada–low; Lower Canada, part of what is now called Quebec
bateau, un; un hors-bord, un bateau à moteur–boat; motorboat
beau (masc.), **belle** (fem.)–beautiful, lovely, nice

beaucoup–much, very much
belvédère, le–lookout, nice view
besoin, le; avoir besoin de–need (noun); to have need of, to need
bibliothèque, une–library (for borrowing books)
bien–well
bientôt; À bientôt–soon, very soon; See you soon
bienvenu(e), le/la; la bienvenue–welcome (as a person who is welcome); a welcome
bière, la; la bière in fût–beer; draft beer
bijou, le; une bijouterie–jewel; a jewellery store
billet, le–bill (e.g., a $10 bill), ticket (bus, etc.), note
bistro(t), le–small restaurant, often with liquor licence
blé, le; le blé d'Inde, le maïs; une épluchette de blé d'Inde–wheat; corn, corn on the cob; corn boil or roast
bleuets, les (masc)**; les Bleuets**–blueberries; residents of the Lac St-Jean area
boire: je bois, nous buvons; une boisson–to drink: I drink, we drink; a drink
bois franc, le; les Bois-francs–hardwood; a region of Quebec characterized by hardwood forests
boîte aux lettres, une; une case postal; C.P.–mail box, post box; P.O. box
Bon appétit!–Enjoy your meal!
Bonjour! Allo! (slang)–Good day! Hello, Hi!
Bonsoir! Bonne soirée!–Good evening! Have a good evening!
bord, le; le bord de l'eau–edge, shore; lakeshore
boucherie, une; le boucher–butcher shop; butcher
boulangerie, une; le boulanger–bakery; baker
boutique, la; une boutique hors taxes–shop, boutique; duty-free shop
brasserie, une–pub, tavern

brouillard, le; risque de brouillard–fog; risk of fog
bureau, le–office
bureau de poste, le–post office
Ça va bien?–How's it going? Everything all right?
cadeau, un; une boutique de cadeaux–gift; gift shop
café, le; un café–coffee, coffee shop
caisse populaire Desjardins, la, la Caisse Pop–credit union, member of a Quebec bank
canton, le; les cantons de l'est–township; the Eastern Townships
carte de crédit, la–credit card
carte, la; la carte routière–map; road map
casque, le; la casquette–helmet;; baseball cap
casse-croûte, le–canteen
Cédez–Yield (a road sign, usually triangular)
CEGEP, Collège d'Enseignement Général et Professionnel–college, a junior college
ceinture, la; une ceinture fléchée–belt; multicolored sash, often hand-woven
centre-ville, le–downtown
centre d'achats, le (anglicism); **un centre commercial**–shopping centre
chambre, la, une pièce; une chambre à coucher–room; a bedroom
champ de bataille, le–battlefield
charcuterie, une–delicatessen
chasse, la–hunting
chaud(e); il fait chaud–warm; it is warm
chauffeur, le–driver, chauffeur
chemin de fer, le–railway (literally, the iron road)
chemin, le; le chemin du Roy (roi) aussi Route 138–road; the King's road, also Route 138
chevreuil, un; un cerf de Virginie–deer
chez nous; chez mon père; chez moi–home, at our

home; at my father's; at my place
chien, le; la chienne–dog
chute, la; les chutes–waterfall; falls
cinéma, le–movie theatre
circulation, la; circulation locale seulement–traffic; local traffic only
CLSC, Centre Local des Services Communautaires–local health clinic
Combien?–How much?
Comment?–How?
Comment ça va?–How are you? How are things?
composer: composez–to dial (a telephone number); (you) dial
comprendre; je ne comprends pas; comprenez-vous?–understand; I don't understand; do you understand?
comptant; payez comptant–cash (i.e., not credit card); pay cash
conquête, la; la Conquête–conquest; the Conquest (the British victory in Quebec in 1759)
côte, la; la Côte Nord–hill, coast, shore (also rib as in steak); North Shore
courrier, le–mail, letters
crevaison, la; la flat (anglicism)–flat tire
cul-de-sac, le–dead-end street
danger, le; Danger–danger
défense de fumer; . . .passer; . . .flâner–No smoking; . . . trespassing; . . . loitering
dégel, le–thaw
déjeuner, le–breakfast
demain–tomorrow
dentiste, le; la dent; les dents; le dentier–dentist; tooth; teeth; denture
dépanneur, le–corner store, "the depp"
départ, le–departure, departure time, start line

dépôt, un; déposer–deposit (in a bank); to deposit
désolé(e)–sorry
détroit, le–strait
Dieu; mon dieu!–God; my lord!
dimanche, le; en abrégé, dim–Sunday, abbrev. Sun.
dîner, le–lunch
disponible–available
douanes, les (fem.)–customs, customs office
drapeau, le; le fleur de lis; l'unifolié–flag; flag of Quebec; flag of Canada (the Maple Leaf)
droit(e) (adj.)**; tout droit**–straight; straight ahead
droite, la; à droite–right; keep to the right
Dynamitage—fermez votre émetteur–Dynamite zone—shut off your transmitter, radio
eau, l' (fem.)–water
école, une; un(e) écolier, -ière–school; schoolchild
economusée, une–small museum which may sell products it creates
église, une; une église catholique–church; a Catholic church
encan, l' (masc.)–auction
enregistrement, l' (masc.)–registration
entrée, l' (fem.)**; entrée interdite**–entrance, an appetizer (on a menu); do not enter, no entry
épicerie, l' (fem.)–grocery store
équestre (adj.)**; le centre équestre**–equestrian; a riding centre
érable, un; l' érablière (fem.)–maple; sugar bush, where they make maple syrup and sugar in early spring
escalade, l' (fem.)–climbing
escalier, l' (masc.)**; l'escalier roulant**–stairs, staircase; escalator
est, l' (masc.), **E**–east
étage, un; le premier étage–floor; the first floor

above the ground floor

été, l' (masc.); **en été**–summer; in summer

être: je suis, tu es, il est, nous sommes, vous êtes, ils sont–to be; I am, you (sing.) are, he is, we are, you (pl.) are, they are

étudiant(e)–student

facture, la–invoice; the bill, e.g., in a restaurant

faune, la–fauna, native animal life

fermer: fermé(e)–to close: closed

fin, la; la fin des voies rapides–end; end of express lanes

fleur, la; la fleur de lis; le fleurdelisé–flower; fleur-de-lis; the Quebec flag

fleuve, le; le St-Laurent–river flowing to the ocean; the St. Lawrence

flore, la–flora, native plant life

forêt, la–forest

forfait, un; le prix forfaitaire–package deal, contract; cost of a package deal

foyer, le–home, retirement home, fireplace

français(e); le français, la langue française–French; the French language

froid(e); j'ai froid; les mains froides; il fait froid–cold; I am cold; cold hands; it's cold (weather)

frontière, la; la frontière américaine–border; the American border

gabarit, le–clearance

garagiste, le–garage owner or mechanic

garçon, le–boy; waiter

garderie, la; la gardienne–day-care (place); baby-sitter

gare de chemin de fer, la, la gare–railway station

gauche; à gauche; la gauche–left, awkward; to the left; the left

geler; gelé(e)–freeze; frozen

Gendarmerie Royale du Canada, la; la GRC–Royal Canadian Mounted Police; RCMP
gérant, le–manager
gîte touristique, le; le gîte du passant–bed and breakfast establishment
glace, la; un glaçon–ice; ice cube, icicle
glisser: je glisse; une glissade–to slide: I am sliding; a slide
gratuit(e), gratis; entrée gratuite–free, without charge; free entry
guichet automatique, le, les services automatisés–automatic teller, bank machine
hebdo, un, l'hebdomadaire–weekly newspaper
héberger; l'hébergement (masc.)–to lodge, shelter; lodging
heure, l' (fem.)–hour, the time
hier; avant-hier–yesterday; day before yesterday
homard, le–lobster
hôpital, l' (masc.)–hospital
horloge, une (fem.)–clock
hôtel, un; l'hôtel de ville, la mairie–hotel; town hall
huard, un; un loonie–loon; the one-dollar coin
huile, l' (fem.); **vérifiez l'huile, s'il vous plaît**–oil; check the oil, please
immeuble, l' (masc.); **immobilier, -ière** (adj.)–real estate
interdire: interdit(e)–prohibit, forbid: prohibited
jardin, le; le jardin botanique–garden; botanical garden
jeudi, le; en abrégé, jeu–Thursday, abbrev. Thurs.
jour, un–day
journal, le; les journaux–newspaper; newspapers
journée, une; Bonne journée!–day; Have a good day!
kiosque, le–newsstand, flower stand, fruit stand

lac, le; le bord du lac–lake; lakeshore
lentement–slowly
librairie, la–bookstore
libre–free; vacant, available
ligne, la; la ligne d'arrêt; la ligne de gel–line; stop line (at an intersection); frost line
logiciel, le—computer program
loisir, un–leisure activity
louer: je loue, nous louons; à louer–to rent: I rent, we rent; for rent, for lease
lundi, le; en abrégé, lun–Monday; abbrev. Mon.
M; Mme; Mlle–Mr.; Mrs.; Miss
maîtres chez nous–masters in our own house
marché aux puces, le–flea market, garage sale
mardi, le; en abrégé, mar; Mardi Gras–Tuesday; abbreviated Tues.; Shrove Tuesday
marée, la; la marée haute; la marée basse–tide; high tide; low tide
matin, le; quatre heures du matin–morning; four o'clock in the morning
maudit!–damn! curses!
mer, la–sea, ocean
merci; merci beaucoup–thank you; thank you very much
mercredi, le; en abrégé, mer–Wednesday; abbrev. Wed.
météo, la; météorologique (adj.)–weather forecast; meteorological
Métro, le–the Metro, the Montreal subway
midi, le; à midi–noon; at noon
minuit, le; il est minuit–midnight; it's midnight
Minute!; dans quelques minutes–Wait a minute; in a few minutes
monnaie, la–money, change (coins)
mont, le; la montagne–mountain

motoneige, la–snowmobile
moulin, le; un moulin à blé; un moulin à scie (or **la scierie); un moulin à vent**–mill; grist or grain mill; sawmill; windmill
musée, le–museum
nager: je nage; un nageur, une nageuse–swim: I swim; swimmer
neige, la; une tempête de neige; un flocon de neige–snow; snowstorm; snowflake
NIP, le numéro d'identification personelle–PIN, personal identification number (at ATM machine)
nom, le; le nom de fille; le prénom; le nom de famille–name; maiden name; first name; family name
nord, le; le Grand-Nord–north; the Far North
orage, un–storm
ordinateur, un–computer
où? Où suis-je? Où est-il?–where? Where am I? Where is he?
ouest, l' (masc.), **O**–west
ouvert(e) (adj.)**; ouvert quand les feux clignotent**–open; open when the lights are flashing
page, la; les pages jaunes–page; yellow pages
paiement direct, le–debit card payment
palourde, la–clam (seafood)
papeterie, la–office supply store, stationery shop
parc, le; l'auto-parc (masc.)–park, playground; parking lot
Pardon? Excusez-moi, je m'excuse–Pardon me? (I didn't hear you); Excuse me
parler: je parle, tu parles, il parle; parlez-vous l'allemand?–to speak: I speak, you speak, he speaks; do you speak German?
patron, le–the boss
pêche, la; la pêche blanche, la pêche sur glace–

fishing; ice fishing

pension, une, un foyer–home (usually for seniors)

pente, une; une pente de ski; un remonte-pente–slope; ski slope; ski lift

permis, le; le permis de conduire–permit, license; driver's license

phares, les (masc.)**; Vos phares?**–headlights; Did you leave your lights on? (at the end of a tunnel)

pharmacie, une–drugstore, medicine cabinet

piscine, une–swimming pool

piste, la; une piste cyclable; une piste de ski–trail, path, track; bicycle path; ski trail

plage, la; la serviette de plage–beach; beach towel

pluie, la; la pluie verglacée, le verglas–rain; freezing rain

pneu, le; un pneu à neige; les pneus quatre saisons–tire; snow tires; four-season tires

pont, le; un pont couvert–bridge; covered bridge

port, le–port (harbor)

porte, la–door

portefeuille, le–briefcase

porte-monnaie, la–wallet

poste, la; le bureau de poste–mail; post office

pour–for

Pourquoi?–Why?

pourboire, le–tip (for waiter)

poutine, la–poutine (mixture of cheese curds, French fries and gravy)

Préparez-vous à arrêter–Be prepared to stop

preuve d'assurance, la–proof of insurance

printemps, le–spring (season)

priorité de virage au clignotement du feu vert–you may turn left when the green light flashes

prochain(e) (adj.); **à la prochaine**–next; till the next time

quai, le–wharf, pier, platform (in bus or train station)
Quand? À quelle heure?–When? At what time?
quelque(s)–some, any
Qui?; Qui est là?–Who?, Whom?; Who is there?
quincaillerie, une–hardware store
Quoi?–What?
ralentir: ralentissez!–to slow down; slow down!
rang, un–range road, a country road
reculez!–go back, back up!
remorquer; le remorquage, le towing (anglicism)–to tow; towing (a car)
rendez-vous, le–appointment
renseignement(s), le(s); information touristique; ?–information; tourist information; ?
réserve faunique, la–wildlife reserve
restaurant, le; une salle à manger–restaurant; dining room
réunion, la–meeting
revue, la–magazine, review
rez-de-chaussée, le; RC–ground level, street level, main floor; on elevator button for main floor
rire: je ris, nous rions; un rire–to laugh: I laugh, we are laughing; a laugh
risque, le; risque de brouillard–risk; risk of fog
rive, la; la Rive-sud–shore; the South Shore
rivière, la–river (flowing into river or lake)
route, la; Route 112–road, track; Highway 112
rue, la; rue barrée–street, road; road is blocked
ruisseau, le–stream, brook
saison, la; saisonnier, -ière–season; seasonal
salle, la; la salle d'attente; la salle d'urgence–room; waiting room; emergency room
samedi, le; en abrégé, sam–Saturday; abbrev. Sat.
seigneur, le; la seigneurie–lord of the manor; land

grant of the French regime

semaine, la; la semaine prochaine; la semaine passée–week; next week; last week

sens unique, le–one way (e.g., a one-way street)

sentier, le; le sentier pédestre–trail; walking or hiking trail

ski alpin, le; le ski de fond–alpine skiing; cross-country skiing

société, la; la Société des alcools–company; provincial government liquor and wine store

solde, le–balance, a bank balance; sale at reduced prices

sortie, la; les trois prochaines sorties–exit; next three exits

souper, le–supper, dinner in the evening

sous-sol, le; SS–basement; on elevator button

souterrain, souterraine (adj.)–underground, e.g., streets or tunnels

spiritueux, les (masc.)–liquor, spirits

station service, la; un poste d'essence–gas station

stationnement, une aire de; stationner–parking area; to park

stopper; stop; le feu rouge–to stop; stop; stop light

sud, le; S–south

Sûreté du Québec, la; la SQ–Quebec police force

surveillance aérienne, la–aerial surveillance

tabagie, une–tobacconist, newsstand

tarif, le–rate, cost, price

taxe de vente du Québec, la; la TVQ–Quebec sales tax; QST

taxe sur produits et services, la; la TPS–goods and services tax; GST

tempête; tempête de neige–windstorm; snowstorm

temps, le; Quel temps fait-il?–time, weather;

What's the weather like?

terrain, le; un terrain de golf–ground; golf course

théâtre, le; le théâtre d'été–theatre; summer stock theatre

timbre, un–stamp for mailing letters

toilette, la; faire sa toilette–toilet, washroom; to get washed and dressed

tout(e), tous, toutes–all, every

Toutes taxes incluses–All taxes included

traverser: je traverse, nous traversons; le traversier–to cross: I am crossing, we cross; ferry, ferryboat

trop; bien trop–too, too much; much too much

urgence, l' (fem.); **Urgences Santé**–emergency; ambulance service in Montreal

Va-t'en! (sing.), **Allez-vous-en!** (pl.)–Go away!

vedette, la; en vedette–star (of film); starring

vendre: je vends, nous vendons; à vendre–to sell: I am selling, we are selling; for sale

vendredi, le; en abrégé, ven–Friday; abbrev. Fri.

vente, la; une vente de garage–sale; garage sale

version française, la; la VF–French version of a film

version originale anglaise, la; la VOA–original English version of a film

vert(e); le vert–green; the green (in golf)

vieux, vieille–old

virage, le; un virage à droite; un virage à gauche–turn; right turn; left turn

vite; Courrez vite!–fast; Run fast!

vitesse, la; la vitesse tue–speed, gear; speed kills

voie, une; voie réservée; une voie seulement–lane, way; reserved lane; one lane only

zone d'exploitation contrôlée, la; ZEC–zone of controlled (hunting and fishing) activity

THE MOMS' LITTLE DICTIONARY

ENGLISH–FRENCH

There are several specialized vocabularies in the text:

Useful expressions–Chapter 6, p. 79
Questions & answers–Chapter 6, p. 80-81
To be–**Être**–Chapter 6, p. 81
To have–**Avoir**–Chapter 6, p. 82
Road signs–Chapter 7, p. 90-92
Clothing–Chapter 8, p. 102
Food & restaurants–Chapter 9, p. 122-124
Months and days–Chapter 10, p. 132
Hours and numbers–Chapter 10, p. 133-134
Holidays–Chapter 10, p. 134

actor; actress; comedian–le comédien; la comédienne

adolescent–l'adolescent(e); un(e) ado (slang)

after; afternoon–après; l'après-midi (masc.)

again; Again?–encore; Encore?

age; How old are you?–l'âge (masc.); Quel âge avez-vous?

air conditioning–l'air conditionné (masc.), la climatisation

airplane–l'avion (masc.)

airport–l'aéroport (masc.)

All taxes included–Toutes taxes incluses

all, every–tout(e), tous (masc. pl.), toutes (fem. pl.)

allophone (person whose first language is not

French or English)–l'allophone (masc., fem.)
ambulance–l'ambulance (fem.), Urgences Santé (in Montreal)
also–aussi
anglophone, an English-speaking person–l'anglophone (masc., fem.)
angry; I am angry–fâché(e); je suis fâché(e)
appointment–le rendez-vous
arrival–l'arrivée (fem.), abbrev. arr
auction–l'encan (masc.)
aunt; my aunt–la tante; ma tante
automatic teller; bank machine–le guichet automatique; les services automatisés
autumn, fall–l'automne (masc.)
back up!–reculez!
bad; the weather's awful–mauvais; il fait mauvais
baby; babysitter–le bébé; la gardienne
bachelor, spinster–le/la célibataire
back, behind–arrière, derrière
bakery; baker–la boulangerie; le boulanger
baseball cap; helmet–la casquette; le casque
baseball; at bat; safe; out; an out; infield–le baseball; au bâton; sauf; retiré; un retrait; l'avant-champ (masc.). See also **hit, strike, home run.**
basement–le sous-sol; SS (on elevator buttons)
bath; bathroom; toilet–le bain; la salle de bain; la toilette
battlefield–le champ de bataille
Be prepared to stop–Préparez-vous à arrêter
be: I am, you are, he is, we are, you are, they are–être: je suis, tu es (sing.), il est, nous sommes, vous êtes (pl.), ils sont
beach; beach towel–la plage; la serviette de plage
beautiful, lovely, nice–beau (masc.), belle (fem.)
beaver–le castor

bed; a firm mattress–le lit; un matelas ferme
bed and breakfast–le gîte touristique; le gîte du passant
beer;draft beer–la bière; la bière en fût
before; before coming–avant; avant de venir
belt; multicolored woven sash–la ceinture; la ceinture fléchée
bet, wager (verb)**: I bet, we bet; the bet, the wager**–parier: je parie, nous parions; le pari
bill, e.g. in a restaurant–la facture
bird; birdie, as in badminton–l'oiseau (masc.); le volant (in badminton)
birthday; Happy Birthday!–l'anniversaire (masc.); Bon anniversaire!
bistro, a small restaurant often with a liquor license–le bistro(t)
blacksmith shop, foundry–la forge
blueberries–les bleuets (masc.)
boat; motorboat–le bateau; le hors-bord, le bateau à moteur
body; head; arm; hand; leg; neck; foot; back–le corps; la tête; le bras; la main; la jambe; le cou; le pied; le dos
book; bookstore–un livre; une librairie
border; the American border–la frontière; la frontière américaine
bottom, essence of a question–le fond
boss–le patron
boy–le garçon
breakfast–le déjeuner
bridge; covered bridge–le pont; le pont couvert
briefcase–le portefeuille
brother; brother-in-law–le frère; un beau-frère
buddy, friend–le copain, la copine
butcher shop; butcher–la boucherie; le boucher

buy: I buy, we buy; a purchase–acheter: j'achète, nous achetons; un achat
canoe; kayak–le canot; le kayak
car, automobile–l'auto (fem.), la voiture
carnival–le carnaval
cash (not credit card); pay cash–comptant; payez comptant
cat; kitten–le chat, la chatte; un chaton
catch (verb)**; I catch; catcher**–attraper, recevoir: je reçois; le receveur
celebrity, famous person–le/la célébrité
child; grandchild–un enfant; un petit-enfant
church; Catholic church–une église; l'église catholique
city–la ville
civil servant–le/la fonctionnaire
clam (seafood)–la palourde
climb: I climb, we are climbing–monter: je monte, nous montons
clinic, local health clinic–CLSC, Centre Local des Services Communautaires
clock–l'horloge (fem.)
close: I close; closed–fermer: je ferme; fermé(e)
coat–le manteau
coffee; coffee shop–le café; un café
cold; I am cold; It's cold; a cold day–le froid; j'ai froid; Il fait froid; une journée froide
college, a junior college–un CEGEP, Collège d'Enseignement Général et Professionnel
color: black; white; red; green; yellow; blue; orange–la couleur: noir(e); blanc (blanche); rouge; vert(e); jaune; bleu(e); orange
come; I come; Come!–venir; je viens; Venez!
competition–un concours, une compétition
computer; computer program–l'ordinateur (masc.);

le logiciel
conquest; the Conquest (the British victory in Quebec in 1759)–la conquête; la Conquête
corn on the cob, corn; corn boil or corn roast–le blé d'Inde, le maïs; une épluchette de blé d'Inde
corner store, the depp–le dépanneur
country holiday place–la villégiature
country; land–le pays; le terrain
cousin–le cousin; la cousine
credit card–la carte de crédit
credit union, member of Quebec bank chain–la caisse populaire Desjardins, la Caisse Pop
cross: I cross, we cross–traverser: je traverse, nous traversons
customs office–les douanes (fem.)
dam (e.g., a hydroelectric dam)–le barrage
damn! curses!–maudit!
dance: I am dancing; do you want to dance?–danser: je danse; voulez-vous danser?
daughter-in-law–une bru
day; Have a good day!–un jour; Bonne journée!
dead end street–le cul-de-sac
deer–un chevreuil; le cerf de Virginie
delicatessen–la charcuterie
dentist–le dentiste
departure–le départ
deposit (noun); **deposit** (verb)–un dépôt; déposer
dial: (you) dial (a telephone number)–composer: composez
difficult–difficile
direct payment by debit card–le paiement direct
disgusting–dégueulasse, dégueu (slang)
dive: I dive; diver–plonger: je plonge; le plongeur, la plongeuse
doctor–le médecin, le docteur

dog–le chien, la chienne
door–la porte
downtown–le centre-ville
dress–la robe
dress; dress oneself–habiller; s'habiller
drink (verb): I drink, we drink; a drink–boire: je bois, nous buvons; une boisson
driver, chauffeur–le chauffeur
drugstore–la pharmacie
Dynamite zone—shut off your radio transmitter–Dynamitage—Fermez votre émetteur
early; you've come early–de bonne heure, tôt; vous venez de bonne heure
ears–les oreilles (fem.)
earth–la terre
east–l'est (masc.), E
edge–le bord
elevator–l'ascenseur (masc.)
emergency; hospital emergency room–l'urgence (fem.); la salle d'urgence
empty (adj.)–vide
end; end of expressway lanes–la fin; la fin des voies rapides
English; the English language–anglais(e); l'anglais (masc.), la langue anglaise
Enjoy your meal!–Bon appétit!
Enjoy yourself!–Amusez-vous bien!
enough–assez
entrance; do not enter, no entry–l'entrée (fem.); entrée interdite
equestrian (adj.)**; horse-back riding centre**–équestre; le centre équestre
escalator–l'escalier roulant (masc.)
evening; Good evening!–le soir, la soirée; Bonsoir! Bonne soirée!

except for; with the exception of–excepté; à l'exception de
excuse me–excusez-moi, je m'excuse
exit; next three exits–la sortie; les trois prochaines sorties
expressway, autoroute–l'autoroute (fem.)
face; forehead; eye, eyes; eyebrow; nose; mouth; lips; cheek; chin–la figure; le front; l'oeil, les yeux (masc.); le sourcil; le nez; la bouche; les lèvres (fem.); la joue; le menton
family–une famille
farm–la ferme
fast; faster–vite; plus vite
father; grandfather; father-in-law–le père; le grand-père; le beau-père
fauna, native animal life–la faune
feast; the Quebec National Day (June 24)–la fête; la Fête nationale
ferry, ferryboat–le traversier
festival–le festival
fill-up; fill it! (with gas)–le plein; faites le plein
fire; fireworks–le feu; les feux d'artifice
fish; fish shop–le poisson; la poissonnerie
fishing; ice fishing–la pêche; la pêche blanche, la pêche sur glace
flag; flag of Quebec; flag of Canada–le drapeau; le fleurdelisé; l'unifolié (masc.)
flat tire–la crevaison; la flat (an anglicism)
flea market; garage sale–le marché aux puces; la vente de garage
floor; main floor; the first floor up–un étage; le rez-de-chaussée; le premier étage
flora, native plant life–la flore
flour; flour or wheat mill–la farine; moulin à farine, moulin à blé

flower–la fleur
fog; risk of fog–le brouillard; le risque de brouillard
foliage–le feuillage
foot; on foot–le pied; à pied
footwear; shoe–les chaussures (fem.); le soulier
forest–la forêt
formal attire–la tenue de soirée
francophone, French-speaking person whose mother tongue is French–le/la francophone
free, available–libre
free; without charge; free entry–gratuit, gratis; sans frais; entrée gratuite
freeze; frozen; my ears are frozen–geler; gelé(e); mes oreilles sont gelées
French version of a film–la version française; VF
French; the French language–français(e); le français, la langue française
Friday, abbrev. Fri.–le vendredi; en abrégé, ven
friend; friendship–l'ami(e); l'amitié (fem.)
front page of a newspaper–la une
game; out of play, offside–le jeu; hors jeu
garageman; garageman's language–le garagiste
garden; botanical garden–le jardin; le jardin botanique
gas station–la station service; le poste d'essence
gift; gift shop–le cadeau; une boutique de cadeaux
girl, daughter; Wards of the King; little girl–la fille; les Filles du Roy; une fillette
glove–un gant
Go away!–Allez-vous-en!
go to bed; Go to bed!–se coucher; Allez-vous coucher!
go: I am going, we go; Let's go!–aller: je vais, nous allons; Allons-y!
goal (hockey); base (baseball)–un but
goalie–le gardien

God; my lord!–Dieu; mon Dieu!
gold (mineral), gold medal–l'or (masc.)
golf (noun); **golfer; golf course**–le golf; un golfeur, une golfeuse; le terrain de golf
Goodbye! Till we meet again!–Au revoir!
Good day! Hello!, Hi!–Bonjour! Allo! (slang)
goods and services tax; GST–la taxe sur produits et services; la TPS
goose; snow goose–l'oie; l'oie blanche (fem.)
green; the green (in golf)–vert; le vert
grocery store–l'épicerie (fem.)
ground; ground floor–le terrain; le rez-de-chaussée
gulf (of a river)–le golfe
hair (of the head)–les cheveux (masc.)
hand; finger; toe–la main; le doigt; l'orteil (masc.)
hardwood; a region of Quebec characterized by hardwood forests–le bois franc; les Bois-francs
hardware store–la quincaillerie
hat; tuque–le chapeau; la tuque
have: I have, you have, he has, we have, you have, they have–avoir: j'ai, tu as (sing.), il a, nous avons, vous avez (pl.), ils ont
head; headache–la tête; le mal de tête
headlights; Did you leave your lights on?–les phares (masc.); Vos phares?
health; health break–la santé; la pause santé
heart–le coeur
heat, warmth–la chaleur
Hello!–Bonjour! Allo! (slang)
Here is, here are; there is, there are; Here I am!–Voici! Voilà! Me voici!
hill, coast, shore–la côte
him; himself–lui; lui-même
hit; a hit (in baseball)–un coup; un coup sûr
hitchhike–l'auto-stop (masc.); faire du pouce

hockey–le hockey
hold (noun)**; capture; hit (baseball)**–une prise
home run; a grand slam–un circuit; un grand chelem
home (for seniors)–le foyer, la pension
home, at our home; at my place; home-made pie–chez nous; chez moi; une tarte maison
horse; horseback riding–le cheval; l'équitation (fem.)
hospital–l'hôpital (masc.)
hot; it is hot–chaud(e); il fait chaud
hotel–l'hôtel (masc.)
hour, the time–l'heure (fem.)
house; house wine–la maison; le vin maison
housework; cleaning house; housewife–le ménage; faire le ménage; la ménagère
How much?–Combien?
How's it going? Everything all right?–Ça va bien?
How?; How are you? How are things?–Comment?; Comment ça va?
hunger; I'm hungry–la faim; j'ai faim
hunting–la chasse
hunting and fishing controlled area–une zone d'exploitation contrôlée; ZEC
husband–le mari
ice; ice cube, icicle–la glace; un glaçon
immediately; as soon as possible–aussitôt; aussitôt que possible
information; tourist information, ?–le(s) renseignement(s); l'information touristique (fem.); ?
inn, country inn, small hotel; youth hostel–l'auberge (fem.); l'auberge de jeunesse
invoice (verb)**; the invoice, bill**–facturer; la facture, la note
jewel; a jewellery shop–un bijou; une bijouterie
joy, pleasure; zest for living–la joie; la joie de vivre
key–la clé

know; I know; I don't know; we know how to swim– savoir: je sais; je ne sais pas; nous savons nager
know, be acquainted with; I know him–connaître; je le connais
lake; lakeshore–le lac; le bord du lac
lane, way; reserved lane; one lane only–la voie; la voie réservée; une voie seulement
late–tard, en retard
laugh: I laugh, we are laughing; a laugh–rire: je ris, nous rions; un rire
leaf; maple leaves–une feuille; les feuilles d'érable
lecture, speech–un discours
left; the left; to the left–gauche; la gauche; à gauche
leisure activity–un loisir
less; a little bit less–moins; un peu moins
library–la bibliothèque
lightning; lighting bolts–la foudre; les éclairs
line; stop line (at an intersection); frost line–la ligne; la ligne d'arrêt; la ligne de gel
liquor, spirits–les spiritueux (masc.)
liquor and wine store–la Société des alcools
listen: I listen, we are listening–écouter: j'écoute, nous écoutons
little (adj.)–petit(e)
little (noun)**; a small amount**–un peu; un petit peu
lobster–le homard
lodge, shelter (verb)**; lodging, accommodations–** héberger: l'hébergement (masc.)
lookout, scenic view–le belvédère
loon (bird); one-dollar coin–le huard; un loonie
lose: I lose; he loses; I am lost; she is lost–perdre: je perds; il perd; je suis perdu; elle est perdue
love, like: I love you; love (noun)–aimer: je t'aime; l'amour (masc.)
magazine–la revue

mail box, post box; P.O.–la boîte aux lettres, la case postale; C.P.

mail; post office–la poste, le courrier; le bureau de poste

main floor, street level–le rez-de-chaussée, **RC** on elevator button

make, do: I am doing, we do–faire: je fais, nous faisons

man; gentleman–l'homme (masc.); le monsieur

manager–le gérant

map; road map–la carte; la carte routière

maple sugar; maple syrup–le sucre d'érable; le sirop d'érable

marriage; wedding; married; groom; bride–le mariage; les noces (fem.); marié(e); le marié; la mariée

me; myself–moi; moi-même

medicine (e.g., pills)–les médicaments (masc.)

meeting–une réunion

menu; regular menu; complete meal special–le menu; à la carte; la table d'hôte

Metro (the Montreal subway)–le Métro

milk; dairy bar–le lait; un bar laitier, un comptoir laitier

mill; grist or grain mill; windmill; sawmill–le moulin; le moulin à blé; le moulin à vent; la scierie

minute; five minutes away–une minute; à cinq minutes

mittens–les mitaines (fem.)

Monday; abbrev. Mon.–le lundi; en abrégé, lun

money, change–la monnaie, l'argent (masc.)

month; next month; last month–le mois; le mois prochain; le mois passé, le mois dernier

moose–un orignal

morning; four o'clock in the morning–le matin;

quatre heures du matin
mountain–le mont, la montagne
move back; back up!–reculer; reculez
movie theatre–le cinéma
Mr.; Mrs.; Miss–Monsieur, abbrev. M; Madame, abbrev. Mme; Mademoiselle, abbrev. Mlle
much, very much–beaucoup
museum; small museum which may sell products it creates–un musée; un economusée
name; maiden name; first name; family name–le nom; le nom de fille; le prénom; le nom de famille
near, close; next of kin–proche; les proches
need (noun)**; to need; I need money**–le besoin; avoir besoin de; j'ai besoin d'argent
new–nouveau(x), nouvelle(s)
news (noun)–les nouvelles, les actualités
newspaper; newspapers–le journal; les journaux
newsstand–le kiosque à journaux
next (adj.)**; till the next time**–prochain, prochaine; à la prochaine
night; a night (at a hotel)–la nuit; une nuitée
No smoking; . . . trespassing; . . . loitering–Défense de fumer; . . . passer; . . . flâner
noon; at noon–midi, le midi; à midi
north; the Far North–le nord, N; le Grand-Nord
novel (noun)–un roman
nothing; It's nothing, don't mention it–rien; De rien
number; even; odd–le nombre, le numéro; pair; impair
numeral, digit–le chiffre
nurse, a person who takes care of the sick–l'infirmier, -ière; le/la garde-malade
office–le bureau
office supply store, stationery store–la papeterie
oil; Check the oil, please–l'huile (fem.); Vérifiez

l'huile, s'il vous plaît

old (adj.)–vieux, vieille

one way (a one-way street)–le sens unique

open; open when the lights are flashing–ouvert(e) (adj.); ouvert quand les feux clignotent

original English version (of a film)–la version originale anglaise; VOA

outfitter (for hunters & fishermen)–la pourvoirie

package deal; price of a package deal–un forfait; le prix forfaitaire

pants, trousers–le pantalon

Pardon me? (I didn't hear you); Excuse me–Pardon?; Excusez-moi

parking area; to park–l'aire de stationnement (fem.); stationner

partner–le conjoint, la conjointe

pedestrian–le piéton

pen; pencil–la plume, le stylo; le crayon

people, folks; Quebec's birthday song in French–les gens; Gens du pays

permit, license (noun)**; driver's license**–le permis; le permis de conduire

personal identification number; PIN–le numéro d'identification personnel; NIP

pillow–un oreiller

place (noun)**; chief town, principal town; place of worship**–le lieu; le chef-lieu; le lieu de culte

play: I play; we play; player–jouer: je joue; nous jouons; le joueur

please (verb)**; please?**–plaire; s'il vous plaît?

police (force); Quebec police, the SQ–la police; la Sûreté du Québec, la SQ

popcorn–le maïs soufflé

port (harbor)–le port

post office–le bureau de poste

poster; playing at a theatre–l'affiche (fem.); à l'affiche
price; price tag–le prix; l'étiquette (fem.)
priest; the parish priest–le prêtre
priority turn on flashing green light–priorité de virage au clignotement du feu vert
prohibit, forbid; prohibited–interdire: interdit(e)
proof of insurance–la preuve d'assurance
pub–la brasserie
puck (hockey)–la rondelle
purchase (noun)–un achat
Quebec sales tax; QST–la taxe de vente du Québec; la TVQ
railway–le chemin de fer (literally, the iron road)
railway station–la gare de chemin de fer, la gare
rain; freezing rain–la pluie; la pluie verglacée, le verglas
raincoat–un imperméable
raise (verb); **arise, get up; I'm getting up**–lever; se lever; je me lève
range road, country road–le rang
rate, cost–le tarif
read: I read, he reads, we read, you read–lire: je lis, il lit, nous lisons, vous lisez
reading; reader–la lecture; un lecteur, une lectrice
real estate–l'immeuble (masc.); immobilier, -ière (adj.)
receipt–un reçu
registration–l'enregistrement (masc.)
relatives; parents-in-law–les parents; les beaux-parents
relaxation; to relax (oneself); I'm relaxing–la détente; se détendre; je me relaxe, je me détends
rent: I rent, we rent; for rent, for lease–louer: je loue, nous louons; à louer
restaurant; dining room–le restaurant; la salle à

manger

rib (as in rib steak)–la côte

right; keep to the right–la droite; gardez la droite

river emptying into the sea; the St. Lawrence–le fleuve; le fleuve St-Laurent, le St-Laurent

river (flowing into a lake or river)–la rivière

road; the King's road (Route 138)–le chemin, la route; le chemin du Roy (roi) (Route 138)

rock (very large); Percé Rock–le rocher; le Rocher Percé

room; a bedroom–la chambre, la pièce; une chambre à coucher

room; waiting room; emergency room–la salle; la salle d'attente; la salle d'urgence

roommates–les co-locataires, les co-locs (slang)

Royal Canadian Mounted Police, RCMP–la Gendarmerie Royale du Canada; la GRC

rubber; rubber boots–le caoutchouc; les bottes de caoutchouc

run (verb)**: I run; runner**–courir: je cours; le coureur, la coureuse

sad: I am sad; sadness–triste: je suis triste; la tristesse

sail; sailboat–la voile; le voilier

sale–la vente

salt; pepper–le sel; le poivre

sand; sand dunes–le sable; les dunes de sable (fem.)

Saturday; abbrev. Sat.–le samedi; en abrégé, sam

savings account; chequing account–un compte d'épargne; un compte avec opérations

school; schoolchild; student–une école; un(e) écolier, -ière; un(e) étudiant(e)

score; account–le compte

sea, ocean–la mer, l'océan (masc.)

seal (marine animal)–le phoque

season; seasonal–la saison; saisonnier, -ière
see again; till we meet again; so long–revoir; au revoir; salut! (slang)
see: I see, we are seeing–voir: je vois, nous voyons
self-serve (at a garage)–auto-service, le service libre
sell: I sell, we are selling; for sale–vendre: je vends, nous vendons; à vendre
she, her; herself–elle; elle-même
shop, boutique; duty-free shop–la boutique; une boutique hors taxes
shopping center; go shopping–le centre commercial; faire les emplettes
shore, by the water; the South Shore–la rive, le bord de l'eau; la Rive sud
silver, money; change–l'argent (masc.); la monnaie
sing: I sing, we sing; song; singer–chanter: je chante, nous chantons; la chanson; le chanteur, la chanteuse
skate (noun)**; skating rink; skating**–le patin; la patinoire; le patinage
skiing; alpine skiing; cross-country skiing–le ski; le ski alpin; le ski de fond
ski-tow–le remonte-pente
skunk; smelly animal–la moufette; la bête puante
slide (verb)**: I am sliding; a slide**–glisser: je glisse; une glissade
slope; ski slope–la pente; la pente de ski
slow down: slow down!–ralentir: ralentissez!
slowly–lentement
snack (noun)**; to taste**–un goûter; goûter
snow; snowstorm; snowflake–la neige; une tempête de neige; un flocon de neige
snowman; mascot of the Quebec winter carnival–le bonhomme de neige; Bonhomme Carnaval
snowmobile–la motoneige

some, any; anyone–quelque(s); quiconque
soon, very soon; See you soon; as soon as possible–bientôt; À bientôt; aussitôt que possible
Sorry–Désolé(e)
south–le sud, S
speak: she speaks; do you speak Spanish?–parler: elle parle; parlez-vous l'espagnol?
spouse–un époux, une épouse
spring (season)–le printemps
stairs, staircase–l'escalier (masc.)
stamp (for mailing letters)–un timbre
state; the United States–l'état (masc.); les États-Unis
step (noun)–la marche
stop (noun)**; bus stop; shortstop (baseball)**–l'arrêt (masc.); l'arrêt d'autobus; l'arrêt-court (masc.)
store; department store; shopping–le magasin; le grand magasin; le magasinage
storm; windstorm–l'orage (masc.); la tempête
straight; straight ahead–droit(e) (adj.); tout droit
street, road; blocked road–la rue; la rue barrée
strike (baseball)–une prise
student–un(e) étudiant(e)
suburb, outskirts of a city–la banlieue
sugar bush–l'érablière (fem.)
summer; in summer–l'été (masc.); en été
Sunday; abbrev. Sun.–le dimanche; en abrégé, dim
supermarket–le supermarché
swim: I swim; swimmer–nager: je nage; le nageur, la nageuse
swimming pool–la piscine
tavern–la brasserie, la taverne
tax; all taxes included–la taxe; toutes taxes incluses
team–une équipe
temperature–la température

thank you–merci
thaw–le dégel
theatre; summer stock–le théâtre; le théâtre d'été
them; they; themselves–eux; eux autres; eux-mêmes
there; over there–là; là-bas
thunder–le tonnerre
Thursday; abbrev. Thurs.–le jeudi; en abrégé, jeu
ticket; bill (paper money)–le billet
tide; high tide; low tide–la marée; la marée haute; la marée basse
tie (in sport)–l'égalité (fem.)
tire; snow tire; four-season tires–le pneu; le pneu à neige; les pneus quatre saisons
tired; I'm tired–fatigué(e); je suis fatigué(e)
today–aujourd'hui
together–ensemble
toilet, washroom; to get washed and dressed–la toilette; faire sa toilette
tomorrow–demain
too, too much–trop; bien trop
tooth; teeth; false teeth; toothpaste–la dent; les dents; le dentier; le dentifrice, la pâte à dent
tow (verb)**; towing (a car)**–remorquer; le remorquage, le towing (anglicism)
town hall–l'hôtel de ville (masc.), la mairie
township; the Eastern Townships–le canton; les Cantons de l'Est
toy–un jouet
traffic; local traffic only–la circulation; circulation locale seulement
trail, path, track; bicycle path; ski trail–la piste; la piste cyclable; la piste de ski
trail; walking or hiking trail–le sentier; le sentier pédestre

Tuesday; abbrev. Tues.; Shrove Tuesday–le mardi; en abrégé, mar; Mardi Gras
turn; right turn; left turn–le virage; le virage à droite; le virage à gauche
umbrella–le parapluie
underground (adj.)–souterrain(e)
understand: I don't understand; Do you understand English?–comprendre: je ne comprends pas; Comprenez-vous l'anglais?
Wait a minute; in a few minutes–Minute!; dans quelques minutes
Wait for the signal–Attendez le signal
Waiter; waitress–le garçon; la serveuse
walk (verb)**: I am walking; a step**–marcher: je marche; un pas
wallet–le porte-monnaie
want: I want, he wants, we want–vouloir: je veux, il veut, nous voulons
washing, laundry; doing the wash; washable–le lavage; faire le lavage; lavable
water; a glass of water–l'eau (fem.); un verre d'eau
waterfall; falls–la chute; les chutes
weather–le temps
weather forecast; meteorological–la météo; météorologique
Wednesday; abbrev.Wed.–le mercredi; en abrégé, mer
week; next week, last week–la semaine; la semaine prochaine; la semaine passée
weekly newspaper–l'hebdomadaire, l'hebdo
welcome (as, a person who is welcome); Welcome!;You're welcome–le/la bienvenu(e); Bienvenue!; bienvenue, de rien
well; All right!–bien; Bien!
west–l'ouest (masc.), O
whale–la baleine

wharf, pier–le quai
What?–Quoi?
When? At what time?–Quand? À quelle heure?
Where? Where am I ? Where is he?–Où? Où suis-je? Où est-il?
Who? Whom?; Who is there?–Qui?; Qui est là?
Why?–Pourquoi?
wildlife reserve–la réserve faunique
window–la fenêtre
windshield–le pare-brise
windshield washer fluid–le lave-glace
windshield wiper–l'essuie-glace (masc.)
winter; in winter–l'hiver (masc.); en hiver
without–sans
woman–une femme
wool; pure wool–la laine; pure laine
work term–le stage
world; of the world–le monde; mondial(e) (adj.)
year; Happy New Year!–l'année (fem.); Bonne Année!
year; next year; last year–l'an (masc.); l'an prochain; l'an passé
yesterday; day before yesterday–hier; avant-hier
Yield (road sign)–Cédez
young; a young person; youth–jeune; un(e) jeune; la jeunesse
zoo–le jardin zoologique

ABOUT THE AUTHORS:

Heather Keith-Ryan

Heather Keith-Ryan was born and raised in Montreal. She earned her BSc in Honours Chemistry from the University of Montreal in 1968. After working as a chemist and teaching high school, she moved to the Eastern Townships of Quebec with her family to a small farm in South Stukely. Raising sheep and children were her principal preoccupations, but politics attracted her and she was elected to the municipal council in South Stukely in 1970. She served as town councillor for six years, between working as municipal building and septic tank inspector and becoming secretary-treasurer. In 1985 she bought a Georgian house in Mansonville near the Owl's Head ski center and opened a Bed and Breakfast. In 1987 she became a licenced real estate agent working with Stuart Realties in Knowlton. In the same year she was acclaimed president of Townshippers Association, an English-language lobby group. She resigned the post in 1989 to run as an independent candidate in the provincial election. She was elected municipal councillor in the township of Potton in 1989 and served four years. Heather made presentations as an individual to the Bélanger-Campeau Commission in 1990 and to the Commission sur l'Avenir du Québec in 1995. She is a volunteer in many organisations.

Sharon McCully

Sharon McCully began her career in journalism eighteen years ago as a community newspaper reporter with the Gaspé's weekly newspaper SPEC. She is now the Knowlton bureau chief for the daily *Record* and the weekly *Brome County News.* She is a former president and current director of the Quebec Community Newspaper Association and a member of the executive of the Canadian Community Newspapers Association, an organization representing 680 community newspapers. While president of QCNA she hosted a linguistic duality seminar for French and English language editors and publishers from across Quebec and Canada. In 1993 she chaired the national community newspaper convention, bringing some 350 Canadian newspaper editors and publishers and their families to Quebec. She is a regular correspondent for CBC's radio program Quebec AM, reporting from Knowlton, and her stories have appeared in the *Gazette* (Montreal), the *Globe and Mail* (Toronto) and numerous other newspapers and magazines. She has served as a volunteer on a wide range of boards and associations. She is married with five children.

Heather and Sharon met more than a decade ago as presidents of the English-language associations in the Eastern Townships and the Gaspé respectively at a meeting of minority-language associations in Ottawa.

STATISTICAL SUMMARY & GENERAL INFORMATION

Population: Canada (1995 projection): 29,606,100
Quebec (1995 projection): 7,329,900 (24.76%)

Quebec: English home language: 10.5%
French home language: 82.5%
Multiple home languages : 7.0%

Largest cities:	Population:
Montreal (island)	1,900,000
Quebec City region	500,000
Laval (island)	350,000
Hull–Gatineau region	200,000
Chicoutimi–Jonquière	160,000
Sherbrooke & region	140,000
Trois-Rivières and region	136,000

Population density: 4.39 residents per sq. km.
11.38 residents per sq. mi.

Area: 644,000 sq. mi./1,667,926 sq. km.

Average snowfall: 300 cm/118 in.

Avg. temperature: January: –17°C to –7°C / 1°F to 19°F
July: 17°C to 30°C / 69°F to 90°F

Capital city: Quebec City

Roads: 20,000 km (12,400 mi.)

Highest point accessible by road: Mont Megantic in the Eastern Townships (2200 m/3610 ft)

Airports:

- Montreal: Dorval—domestic, U.S. & internat'l flights
  Mirabel—charter and cargo flights
  Toll-free information for both Montreal airports from Quebec and area code 613: 1-800-465-1213
- Quebec City (not all carriers)

Quebec tourist information: available in Quebec, elsewhere in Canada and the United States: 1-800-363-7777.

Parks Canada in Quebec: 1-800-463-6769 (in Canada only)

Quebec parks and wildlife reserves: toll-free number in Quebec, Ontario and the eastern U.S.: 1-800-665-6527

Emergency phone number in most cities and towns: 911

Postal rates (Mar. 1996): 45¢ + 7¢ tax for 30 gm/1 oz letter or postcard in Canada; 52¢ + 8¢ tax for same to US

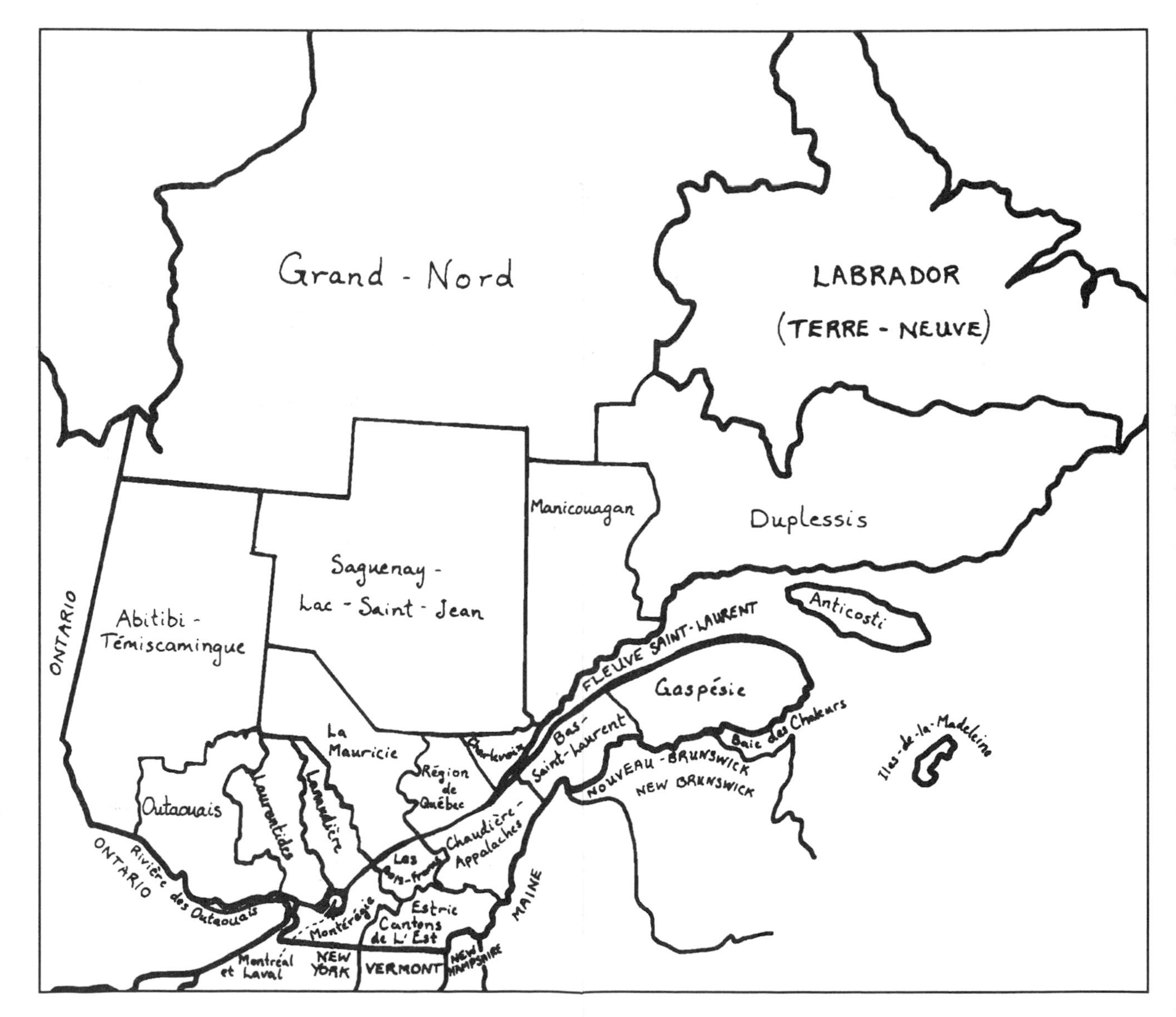

Quebec: Bonjour, eh?

Do you know someone who would like to know more about Quebec, or who would enjoy a visit here with an introduction like **Quebec: Bonjour, eh?** You can order a copy or copies at a special price with the coupon below.

Bonus offer—for every 20 copies you order, you will receive a complimentary copy.

Have you read **Quebec: Bonjour, eh?** and felt that there was something that should have been included? If so, please tell us about it. Send in the coupon below, and if we include your suggestion(s) in the next edition, we'll send you a free copy.

Please send me [ ] copies of **Quebec: Bonjour, eh?** at $15.00 (Canadian) each, including postage and GST. I enclose a cheque or money order payable to **VOA Publications Reg'd** in the amount of [$] Canadian. (Call or write for U.S. offer.)

Name ______________________________

Address ______________________________

City or town ______________________________

Province or State ________________ Postal code __________

Vocabulary or information I would like to see in the book:

(Continue on the other side if you have a lot to tell us.)

Send to:

VOA Publications Reg'd
Box 404
Mansonville, Quebec
J0E 1X0

or

Quebec: Bonjour, eh?
c/o The Record
Box 488, Knowlton
Quebec J0E 1V0